CONTRADICTIONS AND DILEMMAS
Studies on the Socialist Economy and Society

Contradictions and Dilemmas

Studies on
the Socialist Economy
and Society

by
János Kornai

The MIT Press
Cambridge, Massachusetts
London, England

First MIT Press edition, 1986

Original title:
Ellentmondások és dilemmák,
Budapest, Magvető, 1983

Published in Hungary by Corvina Kiadó, 1985

Translated by:
Ilona Lukács, Julianna Parti, Brian Mclean, and György Hajdú

© János Kornai, 1983, 1985

Library of Congress Cataloging in Publication Data

Kornai, János.
  Contradictions and dilemmas.

  Translation of: Ellentmondások és dilemmák.
  Bibliography: p.
  1. Hungary—Economic conditions—1968— —Addresses, essays, lectures. 2. Economics—Addresses, essays, lectures. 3. Marxian economics—Addresses, essays, lectures. I. Title.
HC300.28.K67213   1986   330.9439'053   85-5168
ISBN 0-262-11107-1

Contents

Preface to the American Edition

This book is the translation of a volume published originally in the Hungarian language. It is addressed not only to the professional academic economist, but also to the general reader. The essays are therefore written in a style accessible to a wider set of readers interested in the issues of socialism and system comparison.

The volume sold out in my country within a few weeks. Perhaps this is because the Hungarian reader, even if he does not agree with the author's conclusions, is surely tormented by the contradictions and dilemmas discussed in the book. He knows the issues analyzed in these essays from first-hand experience. I view with some trepidation the issuing of an American edition. Will American readers, without the same first-hand experience and with a different historical and cultural tradition, be interested at all? Should they be?

One motivation for reading the book can be intellectual and political curiosity. There are now 27 socialist countries in the world: all together 1.7 billion people live under this political and economic system. No one can be indifferent to the state of affairs in socialist economies. This small volume of seven essays does not aim at a broad description and analysis of socialist systems; this ambitious task is left to monographs. But it tries to throw some light on a few important characteristics of social economies. Gathered here then are the observations of an inside witness, one who tries to be as frank and impartial as possible.

The essays distinguish the "classical" or "traditional" form of a highly centralized socialist economy from a system that is in the process of institutional reforms. On the cover of the Hungarian edition a test tube is shown and in the tube there is the map of Hungary. Yes—Hungary is in a state of permanent experimentation. It is a guinea pig of history—How far can the renewal of a socialist economy go? The experiment has proceeded for some 28 years now. Friends and enemies of socialism must be equally interested to learn about the experiences of the reform. This book does not give a straightforward answer to the ultimate questions of reformed socialism, but at least it tries to offer some critical analyses.

Although the volume's focus is on socialist systems, a recurrent theme is comparison between socialist and capitalist systems, sellers' and buyers' markets, centralized and decentralized management. I hope this book will provide some food for thought and help the American reader to understand the deep differences and also to discover the similarities and analogies between the systems.

As for the differences, the pure models of classical capitalism and classical socialism are symmetrically antithetical: for instance, private versus public ownership, decentralized versus centralized decision-making associated with characteristic dichotomous consequences, the predominant role of price signals versus the predominant role of non-price signals, the buyers' versus the sellers' market, and so on. Real modern societies are, however, different from the pure models of theory. They are combinations and mixtures of the features listed above. Therefore quite a few phenomena which occur widely and intensively in socialist countries also appear in the highly developed industrial market economies and in the non-socialist Third World countries, at least in some segments of the system and to a certain degree. Let me mention three issues discussed in this book: shortages, the paternalistic role of the state vis-à-vis weak producers, and bureaucratic management. I wonder whether these are topics completely unfamiliar to the American reader? He experienced shortages and rationing during the World Wars, and more recently, and briefly, during the oil shocks of the 1970s. Today in some sectors—rent-controlled housing and in some areas of the health services, for instance—there can be a certain deficit of resources. The American reader is also a regular witness to political struggles; lobbying and pressuring for and against the paternalistic role of the state in supporting and sheltering ailing sectors and weak producers. As for bureaucratic control and expandable, "soft" budget constraint, there are the well-known stories of defense expenditures, military investments, and federal and local subsidization of other bureaucratic organizations. I do not want to overrate the similarities, or the differences. The aim of these essays is just to stimulate comparative thinking.

I am aware that all generalizations about citizens of a particular country are inevitably superficial. Nevertheless I am risking just that in confronting a rather typical American and Hungarian attitude. Many Americans in public life and politics, as well as in the academic world, have a very deeply embedded belief: that every problem has a solution. Many Hungarians, at least in intellectual circles, do not share this belief. Not because we know it better from mathematics, which provides many examples of unsolvable problems; rather it is more a question of *Weltanschauung* generated by historical and cultural tradition. There are unsolvable dilemmas, because each of us has conflicting goals and adheres to conflicting ethical postulates. This volume contains essays on such issues. Life, of course, produces pragmatic compromises, and rightly so—but at least we should bravely face the dilemma, before turning to the compromise.

Optimism is the "official party line" in the United States, to use the language of my country. I must warn the reader: this is not an optimistic book. But neither is it pessimistic. There has been a Hungarian tradition for centuries: you are resigned or desperate or angry and a happy outlook is uncertain or improbable—and yet, you work hard and honestly for improvement. Those who have read classics of Hungarian drama or poetry (some are translated into English), or have listened to Bartók's music, will know exactly this contradictory mood. Perhaps a member of a gray and nonphilosophical profession, like that of the economist, can follow the same tradition. Without presenting rosy, utopian prospects, without pretending to know all the optimal solutions, and without hoping for a great breakthrough in the near future, one may still advocate and promote changes for the better.

Cambridge, Massachusetts
April 1985

CONTRADICTIONS AND DILEMMAS
Studies on the Socialist Economy and Society

Introduction*

What is common to the seven studies[1] which make up this volume? First of all, that they have been written by an economist, but *not merely for economists*.[2] They are addressed to all who are interested in economic problems and concerned about social matters. I hope that sociologists, historians, philosophers, lawyers, engineers and officials of political and social organizations will find in them a message worth thinking about.

The *subjects* of the studies have several elements in common. I am mainly concerned with the observation of the *socialist economy* whose functioning I wish to understand and explain. Not the functioning of any *imaginary* socialism, of the kind the first pioneers wished to see or biased propagandists and equally biased counter-propagandists wished to be seen. What I would like to understand is the living *reality* around us.

In my research work I often use the methods of deductive thinking: mathematical models, hypotheses put in an exact form and conclusions deduced strictly from them. But theoretical thinking draws its ultimate inspiration from a generalization of everyday experience. I should be glad if the reader were to sense this in the description of everyday phenomena in this little book: housewives running after articles in short supply, managers begging for subsidies and several other well-known forms of behaviour in economic life. The "regularities" of a socialist economy are not manifestations of normative postulates (the maximum satisfaction of needs, etc.); instead they

* I wish to express my thanks to all those who have helped in publishing this book: the editors, András Nagy Jr, Magda Benczédi, Katalin Farkas and László Boros, and the translators, Ilona Lukács, Julianna Parti, Brian McLean, and György Hajdú. I am very grateful for their attention and care.

are revealed in the behaviour of individuals, groups and organizations. Creating economic theory consists primarily of formulating these regularities exactly and then so combining them as to build up a homogeneous theoretical system, and of elaborating upon certain statements whose truth must be verified. Moreover the criterion for verification is not whether we like a regularity but whether that regularity corresponds with experience.

Comparison is of great assistance in recognizing the specific marks of a socialist economy. Almost all the studies in this book avail themselves of this technique of analysis; some have been written with the express purpose of providing a conceptual system and analytical viewpoints by which systems can be compared. Comparisons have been drawn between the variants of the socialist system (for example, the economy before and after the reform) and between the socialist and capitalist systems. Other dimensions and projections have also been compared. However self-evident the need for comparison may seem, the method is not frequently used in economic theory today. Most researchers specialize in examining a particular system or subsystem. A research economist undertaking to compare systems must be prepared to work out new theoretical categories and cope with serious methodological difficulties instead of using ready-made schemes. Struggles with theoretical and methodological problems are certainly noticeable in the studies included in the present book, and this may cause difficulty to the reader, although it may arouse his intellectual curiosity as well.

The seven studies also share a common *approach*. This has several features, of course. Here I shall mention only the two viewpoints to which attention is also drawn in the title of the book. First, stress is laid on the analysis of the *contradictions* of society, and within society, of the economy. Clearly that is no new discovery. We have all learnt since our schooldays that reality is full of contradictions. The difficulty begins when one takes this thesis, which has grown into a commonplace, seriously and starts to apply it to the examination of our own system. Again in this respect distinctions are worth making. Even orthodox theory admits the existence of contradictions in socialist society arising because the socialist present contains remnants of the capitalist past or the socialist system is surrounded by a capitalist environment. Of course it is still easier to admit the existence of eternal conflicts arising out of the struggles of human society with nature, or the growth and differentiation of needs as the productive forces develop, while the resources available are always scarce by comparison, and so on. These latter types of conflicts have existed and will continue to exist in all periods and under all systems. The conflicts alluded to are touched upon in several places in the book, but attention is centred on the conflicts *generated by socialism itself*. We have the specific intellectual and public task of analysing the nature of the specific conflicts that arise here and only here. That is a task no one else can accomplish in our stead.

By "we" I mean first a wider circle: economists who live in any part of the world under a socialist economic system that allows them a profound insight into how such a system functions. Secondly, I mean to lay particular emphasis on the role of *Hungarian* economists. Due to a number of historical circumstances, we are in a fairly good position to indulge in plain speaking and express critical opinions. Moreover Hungary is in the forefront of experimentation with new economic methods, institutions and mechanisms. Hungary as a laboratory of the history of socialism deserves attention from the outside world, which can perceive as much as filters through the laboratory walls or as much as can be appreciated on a superficial visit. We, economists, are the ones who stand right by the test-tubes. The kinds of experiments carried out, or the timing of them, does not depend on us (although we may exert a degree of influence), but we can at least see at a close range what is taking place in the intricate system of a thousand vessels and pipes, what the instruments and not least the living objects of the experiment indicate.

Quite a few examples are cited in the book of special system-specific conflicts in the socialist economy. The same process that guarantees full employment generates both a shortage of labour and unemployment on the job. The same mechanism that ensures swift economic growth will lead in the long term to phenomena of shortage, to frictions in adjustment and ultimately to the hindrance of growth. Paternalism and a guarantee of the firm's survival are the two aspects of the same phenomenon. Such conflicts do not stem from the faults of a particular manager, from bad planning or a bad style of work. The cause lies deeper than those, in the power structure of society and the form of ownership and institutional system in it. The social sciences have an obligation to face up to all these conflicts and reveal the explanations for them. That is the only way in which they can be combated. (Of course it remains true that new conflicts will then be created.) I have learnt from Marx that the science of socialism must be distinguished from Utopia. Neither deductive logic that starts out from realistic assumptions nor historical experience seem to confirm that we are progressing toward a perfect contradiction-free society. The growing forces of production, technical progress and the transformation of the social conditions may on the one hand improve people's lives and produce important historical achievements, but on the other they may give birth to new conflicts and upheavals, new joys and new miseries.

Here we arrive at the other expression in the title of the book: *dilemmas*. How comfortable it would be if there were only a single path before us, as the adherents of mechanical determinism imagine, or, since we have to choose, if we at least had an accurate compass, an optimum-criterion which was acceptable and even attractive to all, and which told us which path to follow—as the adherents of economy-wide "optimization" consider. Real life, however, places those who must make decisions on matters of greater or lesser importance in a far less comfortable position. "If you choose this, it will be good from a certain point of view, but from another point of view it will be bad." If reality involves contradictions, a decision-maker must inevitably face dilemmas, and that is how the two expressions in the title of this book relate to one another. This thought runs through all the studies like a guiding strand. What I have undertaken to do is not to gloss over the conflicts or reassuringly resolve the dilemmas. I have tried to trace "small" contradictions that show up on the surface back to "big" contradictions hidden in the depths (and even this has been extremely difficult). Thereby I have also tried to trace small, everyday dilemmas back to choices between ultimate values. In everyday economic affairs in the strict sense, such as subsidies for health and housing services or the salaries and bonuses of business executives, are concealed fundamental dilemmas: the conflict between demands that can be made on society and obligations towards society, between security and the stimulation of performance, and a number of other, graver political, social and ethical problems.

The reader of this little book will receive no reassuring answers to his questions. These studies can at the most help him to formulate his questions.

November 1982

NOTES

[1] All the studies in this book were published previously, between 1978 and 1982. Only a few small changes have been made in the texts as previously printed, mainly with a view to avoid overlap. (Even so, a certain amount of overlapping has remained.) The specific message of the studies has been left as it was when originally published.

[2] In the form originally published a few technical terms which may cause difficulties to non-economist readers have been used in the studies. Where these first occur, their meanings have been explained in the notes. As a rule, definitions are not presented, since that would only lead to the use of further technical terms. In preference a paraphrase or illustration to elucidate the meaning of the term has been provided. These explanatory notes inserted by the editors have been marked at the end by an asterisk (*).

The Reproduction of Shortage*

The word *shortage* in the title refers to a well-known group of phenomena that we all encounter as *consumers*. Although in past years the
supply of consumer goods has much improved, "deficit goods" still
keep disturbing smooth supply. Tens of thousands are waiting to get
a telephone station or to buy a car. The gravest shortage phenomenon
in consumption is a housing shortage which has grown into a pressing
social problem.

We keep encountering shortage phenomena not only as consumers
but also as *producers*. Hindrances are not rare in the supply of materials, semi-finished products and parts. Shortage of construction and
installation capacity is conspicuous in investment processes. In addition to all this, labour shortage increasingly retards the expansion of
production.

Many economists and managers think that there are separate phenomena involved. Although symptoms are similar, the causation is
different in each case. One kind of shortage results from the planner's
fault, another one from the negligence of the factory supplying the
product or the trading company that sells them, and a third one may
be the consequence of the price having been fixed too low, etc.

In my opinion all the above-mentioned symptoms spring from the
same root; in the final analysis they can be traced back to common
main causes. We are faced with various concrete manifestations of
the same *general* phenomenon. This study places in the forefront of

* First publication in English: "Resource-constrained versus Demand-constrained Systems",
Econometrica, Vol. 47 (1979), pp. 801–819. Presidential address, presented at the North American and at the European meeting of The Econometric Society, in Chicago, August 29, 1978,
and Geneva , September 6, 1978.

investigation what is common to these various phenomena and the explanations for them.

The "reproduction" of the title refers to the fact that we are not faced with temporary, provisional, occasional events but with a complex of phenomena that constantly reproduces itself under specific circumstances. It is not simply a case of "shortage breeding shortage" although such self-movement and self-generation can also feature. Shortage is continually reborn out of social conditions and certain characteristics of the economic mechanism about which we shall speak in a moment.

The analysis of shortage is a widely diverging subject. Either as a cause or as a consequence, it is interrelated with every important process of economic life. For a comprehensive analysis we ought to go through almost all chapters of economics. This short study does not aim at completeness or at a summary of a longer, more detailed train of thought. It must rest content with confining itself to a fraction of this very large sphere of problems and demonstrating certain important relationships.

Shortage can simultaneously be considered as *good* and *bad*. It is favourable that there is no unutilized capital which is unwanted by any firm for a productive use. There is full employment. (We shall later return to this.) At the same time, achievements are necessarily accompanied by troubles. Shortages cause loss and inconvenience to consumers. They often have to wait for supply, to queue up, and frequently are forced to be content with goods different from their original wish. Sometimes they cannot cover their particular demand at all. Shortage causes disturbances in production. A seller's market develops in which there is not enough incentive for improvement of quality of products and for innovation. All this is mentioned only as a preliminary: my study does not aim either at a normative evaluation, or at elaboration of suggestions. Its exclusive aim is *description* of the phenomenon and *explanation of its causes*.

The examination of shortage present in the socialist economy has numerous precedents in the history of economic thought. Limited space makes it impossible for me to describe them here in detail and to compare my viewpoint with that of others.

I shall carry on the analysis on a rather abstract plane; there will be no detailed representation of economic reality. Basically I treat the "classical" form of a socialist economy, which preceded the economic management reforms of the 1960s and 1970s. I shall not discuss in detail to what extent the momentary state of the Hungarian economic mechanism is identical with, and different from, the "classical" form. A further simplifying assumption I shall make is to disregard foreign trade. I begin my study with the microeconomic approach, and turn to the macroeconomic approach in the second part.

Microanalysis

THE THREE CONSTRAINTS OF INCREASING PRODUCTION

We shall centre attention on the *producer firm,* dealing exclusively with the short-term behaviour of the firm. It is presumed that the firm strives for increasing production, and we shall not question its motivation, i.e. whether its impetus comes from the command of superior authorities, from its own voluntary decision (with a view to increased profit), or from bonuses promised to the managers, or from the urgings of customers, etc.

The question is the following: what are the *constraints* limiting efforts at increasing production? For illustration we can visualize a mathematical programming model of the firm, in which production variables are constrained by inequalities. Many thousands of constraints exist for every firm at any given moment, and, if we keep in mind the totality of firms, i.e. the whole of a national economy, many millions of upper constraints delimit production. Constraints are divided into three large groups:

1. *Resource constraints:* The use of real inputs[1] by production activities cannot exceed the volume of available resources. These are constraints of a *physical* or technical nature: the stock of labour of different qualifications available momentarily for production, the quantity of materials, semi-finished products and parts in stock, the capacity of machines and equipment ready for operation in factories, the usable space in factory premises, and so on.

2. *Demand constraints:* Sale of the product cannot exceed the buyer's demand at given prices.

3. *Budget constraints:* Financial expenses of the firm cannot exceed the amount of its initial money stock and of its proceeds from sales. (Credit will be treated later.)

Which of the three constraints is *effective* is a defining characteristic of the social system. To clarify what is meant by "effective constraint" I should like to refer again to the mathematical theory of inequality system, for instance to linear programming,[2] the use of which is best understood among economists. In the solution of a programming problem, equality holds for some of the constraints which are given originally in the form of inequalities. Production makes use of some resource to a full extent; the sale perhaps extends to the limit of demand; the expenses exhaust the funds available. The constraints for which equality holds are *effective* because they actually delimit the choice. Production would have been greater had the *effective* limits not been reached. However inequality holds for other constraints ("they are not exhausted") in the solution of the programming problem. These are not effective from the point of view of a momentary solution. It is as if they were not there: they are redundant, exerting no influence on the choice.

It is always the comparatively narrower constraints that are effective, for these conflict with the endeavour to raise production. Relatively looser constraints are not effective.

DEMAND-CONSTRAINED AND RESOURCE-CONSTRAINED SYSTEMS

Two "pure" types of systems are discerned from the point of view of effectiveness of constraints. One is the *demand-constrained system*. In it the effective constraint on production increase is the buyer's demand. Demand constraints are narrower than physical resource constraints. The available quantity of resources would allow a further increase of production. Yet producer firms do not avail themselves of this possibility, since they do not see the excess as saleable.

Capitalism is, in its "classical" form, a demand-constrained system. This is the economy *Marx* treats in *Das Kapital* when he writes about the contradiction between the tendency of unlimited expansion of production and the limited purchasing potential of the market.[3]

Keynes's attention was centred on this problem.[4] He analysed the ways in which effective demand can be increased. Governmental and private investments, together with the indirect effects these have on employment and consumers' demand, were among the possibilities he considered.

Modern capitalism—mainly owing to the effect of active state interventions often undertaken in the name of Keynes—can no longer be qualified a "pure" demand-constrained system.

The other "pure" type of system is the *resource-constrained system.* Here the effective constraints to an increase in production are the available physical resources. *A socialist economy is, in its "classical" form, a resource-constrained economy.*[5]

In order to avoid misunderstandings, it should be noted that if an economy is qualified as a resource-constrained system, this does not mean that in such an economy all resources are utilized at 100 per cent at every moment. In production, a more or less strict *complementarity* asserts itself in the short run. Technology is given; various inputs must be combined in fixed proportions. That is, if one of the resources proves to be a bottleneck momentarily, other resources remain partly or fully unutilized at the same time. A number of workers will be idle at the workshop if there is no material to process, or a part is missing for the installation, or there is a power cut; or, on the reverse side, there is material but it is not processed because the worker in charge of the task has not come to work. There is shortage of the resource presenting the bottleneck, and slack of the complementary resources. *Therefore, shortage and slack are not mutually exclusive phenomena, considering the whole of production and a long period, but are necessarily concomitant.*

ON MEASUREMENT

An important conclusion is drawn from the simultaneous presence of shortage and slack. The question of whether any economy is to be qualified as demand-constrained or resource-constrained, cannot be answered by observing its slacks, or its unutilized resources only.

It is possible, but by no means certain, that in comparing two economic systems—one resource-constrained and the other demand-constrained—it must be the former in which the average utilization of resources is higher. The exclusive criterion of distinction is: *what was the effective constraint in the elementary events of production?* If in the overwhelming majority of elementary events demand constraint was effective and physical resources constraint not effective, then we are dealing with a demand-constrained system. If, however, in the overwhelming majority of elementary events the situation was the reverse, i.e. production continually hit physical bottlenecks, the system is qualified as resource-constrained.

This leads us to the problems of *measurement*. Shortage cannot be described by any macro aggregate, and cannot be expressed by adding up the unspent or momentarily unspendable purchasing power of economic units. This is emphatically the case when, with shortage growing chronic, the behaviour of economic units gets somewhat adjusted to the situation. It becomes customary that the product or service desired, but momentarily not available, is substituted for by something else. In this case we say that there is *forced substitution*. Forced substitution and forced spending permanently absorb the purchasing power that its holder cannot spend in accordance with his original purchasing intention. That is why the aggregate "excess demand" measured in money terms is not an operational magnitude.[6]

"Shortage" is the collection of millions of submicro-level elementary shortage events. We shall present a few examples for them. (Here and now, for the sake of completeness, we shall mention non-profit institutions and households besides producer firms.)

(1) Somewhere, some product or service is not available, when the buyer firm, non-profit institution or household wants to buy exactly that product or service exactly at that place.

(2) Some input is not available at the workshop or at the rooms of the non-profit institution, when the firm or non-profit institution would need exactly that input for its activities.

(3) The firm, the non-profit institution or the household effectuates improvised forced adaptation in order to mitigate the consequences of momentary shortage. This may happen either in the course of the purchasing act, or in the course of utilization. For example, a sub-

stitution is made for the missing product or service with a product which is either inferior or more expensive.

In the case of a chronic shortage, thousands or hundreds of thousands of such or similar *elementary shortage events* take place. The *intensity* of shortage depends on the frequency of those elementary shortage events, and also on whether it is only shortage events of comparatively easy consequences that occur frequently, or whether there are also elementary shortage events of grave consequences.

Since this is a stochastic mass phenomenon, it can be described *statistically*. Although each elementary shortage event can be well observed, it is obviously impossible to observe and register all of them without exception. Nevertheless, full measurement can be adequately replaced for practical purposes by observing representative samples and describing the distributions of the main types of characteristic shortage events.

While the intensity of shortage cannot be measured on one summarizing scale, *it has to be described by an ensemble of various shortage indicators*. One shortage indicator or another can show, for instance, the frequency with which a typical shortage event takes place.[7]

Reverting to production, based upon the above, we can use the following two statements as expressions of identical contents: "production often hits resource constraints, i.e. physical bottlenecks", and "the intensity of shortage of inputs in production is high".

HARD OR SOFT BUDGET CONSTRAINT[8]

After the detour concerned with measurement, let us now return to the constraints of production. So far we have not spoken of the third category—the *budget constraint*. In this connection we shall introduce a qualification not customary in microeconomics so far: we shall distinguish between hard and soft budget constraints.

A budget constraint is *hard* if it is asserted with iron discipline: the firm can spend only as much money as it has. It has to cover its expenses from its incomes from sales. It is entitled to take out credit, but the bank is prepared to grant credit only under "conservative" and "orthodox" conditions. This can be, therefore, only an advance for subsequent proceeds from sales.

The budget constraint is *soft,* if the above-mentioned principles do not get asserted consistently.

The hardness or softness of the constraint can be stated indirectly, and through the observation of two phenomena.

First, *survival.* The budget constraint is hard if grave financial difficulties drive the firm to bankruptcy. It dies of its losses in the strict sense of the word, and without regard to whether or not it failed owing to its own negligence, or because of an unfortunate coincidence of external circumstances. The budget constraint is soft if the state helps the firm out of trouble. There are various means to do so: subsidies; individual exemption from the payment of taxes or other charges (their full or partial remission or postponement); allowance on the centrally fixed price of an input; open increase of the centrally fixed selling price or toleration of a hidden price increase; credit granted on soft conditions; prolongation of the due credit repayment, etc. The state is a universal insurance company which compensates the damaged sooner or later for every loss. The paternalistic state guarantees automatically the survival of the firm.

The second phenomenon which allows one to draw an indirect conclusion with regard to hardness or softness of the budget constraint is the *growth* of the firm. The budget constraint is hard if the growth of the firm depends on its own financial position, i.e. on the one hand, on how much it has been able to save and accumulate from its earlier profit, and on the other hand, or whether—under hard, "conservative" conditions—it is ready to take out credit and is able to get credit for investment purposes. This depends on the prospects of its financial situation and the expected profitability of the investment. If the investment proves to be a financial failure, it may lead to bankruptcy of the firm. The budget constraint is soft, if the growth of the firm is not tied to its present and future financial situation. In this case there is no failure; the firm survives even when investment entails grave losses.

What I call here the hardness of the budget constraint is not identical with what is called "profit incentive of the firm" in disputes about economic management reforms in socialist countries. Profit incentive—e.g. profit sharing of managers and workers—is compatible with a soft budget constraint. In such cases managers of the firm ask superior authorities for financial support exactly in order that workers (and maybe also the managers) can get their usual profit share even in the case of losses.

Hard budget constraints are effective in the sense we have explained. They constrain action and the freedom of choice. "We can spend only as much money as we have." "If we invest badly, we shall die of it."

Soft budget constraints are not effective. The financial situation of the firm does not constrain action. Money has only a passive role. "Let it cost what it may." "The main thing is to acquire material and capacity, and money for it will be found in some way." "Once we have a contractor, we shall not stop the investment just because we have no money." "If there is a loss, the state budget will take it over."

The preceding stereotypes of common thought in business circles suggest that the hardness or softness of the budget constraint reflects an *attitude*. It must not be mistaken for the book-keeping category of the balance sheet of the firm. The latter is an *ex post* identity. It is a relationship which holds all the time: the difference of the terminal and the initial money stock is identical with the difference of incomes and of expenses. As opposed to this, the budget constraint—if hard and thereby effective—is an *ex ante* behavioural regularity, which exerts an influence on the firm's decision.

Exactly because it is an *ex ante* constraint, it is related to the firm manager's *expectations*. These are not formed upon the basis of one single event, and develop not only from the manager's experience at his own firm but in the course of a long period, and as a result of generalization of overall experiences. If no firm is ever helped out, or only very rarely rescued from financial failure, the manager will expect the same thing for his own case. He will consider the budget constraint hard and act accordingly. If compensation of losses becomes more frequent, if the growth of the firm starts to break away from its financial situation more often and at more places, the manager of the firm may feel that the probability has grown that his firm would also survive despite exceeding the budget constraint or a financial failure caused by a wrong investment. And, beyond a certain limit, the manager can expect almost with a 100 per cent certainty that the survival of his firm is guaranteed; it can stand every loss and investment financial failure. If the overwhelming majority of firm managers have this expectation for the future, it can be said that the budget constraint is soft.[9]

In the "classic" form of socialist economy the budget constraint is soft. It seems that economic management reforms—although profit-sharing has been introduced in several socialist countries, Hungary among them—have not led to significant hardening of the budget constraint and have not turned it into an effective constraint.

DEMAND OF THE FIRM

There is a close causal relationship between the hardness or softness of the budget constraint and the two groups of constraints discussed earlier: the effectiveness of the resource constraints and of the demand constraints.

Let us take first the case of the *hard* budget constraint.[10] The demand of the firm for inputs depends on the price and the buyer's financial situation. The statements that we know well from standard demand theory are valid if the buyer's budget constraint is hard (and is valid only in that case).[11]

The firm as buyer is prepared *voluntarily* to refrain from purchasing and accumulating too much material, from engaging too many workers, and from starting too large investments—"too many" and "too large" in the sense that in its seller's role the firm may hit a demand constraint, and then the expenses will not be justified subsequently; the firm may suffer losses that may lead to failure in the end. Therefore, the firm must be cautious in determining its demand, because "running away" involves risk and may endanger the existence of the firm.

All this has its multiple effects on interfirm relationships. Every firm is a seller and a buyer at the same time. Demand of the *buyer* firm is constrained by the hard budget constraint. Sales of the *seller* firm, and thereby also its production, are delimited by the buyers' demand constraint. We have arrived at the demand-constrained system.

Aggregate demand can be increased by Keynesian economic policy. Yet as long as the budget constraint remains hard, demand will be *finite*. Even at the Keynesian expansion of demand the investor's risk-aversion is maintained. The system does not expand up to the limits drawn by the bottlenecks of resource constraints.

Let us now turn to the case of the *soft* budget constraint. In that case there is no voluntary constraint on the demand side. Demand is not simply too large, but as a first approximation can be formulated as infinite.

The firm's demand for inputs is price-inelastic. Demand for the firm does not depend on its financial income. Accordingly, the shape of the firm's demand function differs completely from the way it appears in standard microeconomics.

If anything keeps the firm from revealing an "infinite" demand, it is mostly the following two factors: (1) Although it would like to hoard as much material, semi-finished products and parts as possible, capacity of its storerooms is limited. (2) Public opinion and superior authorities condemn "hoarding", including, in addition to the above-mentioned, the "reservation" of labour. It gives a better impression and is therefore better tactics to show some self-restraint in determining demands.

We keep these restraining factors in mind, when we make the following formulation: *the demand of firms for inputs is almost insatiable*. It goes by all means up to the supply limits of inputs. Therefore, in the sphere of inter-firm input-output relationships, the system becomes resource-constrained.

If the budget constraint is soft, Say's principle is not valid, and together with it, Walras's law is not valid either.[12] *In the final result the fundamental axioms of standard microeconomics are not valid. Therein lies the key to understanding the microfoundations of a shortage economy.*

At that point we must conclude the microanalysis. Our discussion contained an extreme amount of simplification; we have no room here for a more thorough and more complete description. In any case the microapparatus is sufficient for examination of a few macro relations.

Macroanalysis

SIMPLIFYING ASSUMPTIONS

I should like to convey what I have to say with the help of a simple model. As a preliminary let me repeat the major assumptions:

1. We shall discuss the "classical" form of socialist economy.
2. A short-term analysis will be made.
3. A stationary economy will be described.[13]
4. Only storable goods will be treated; services will be disregarded.
5. The economy will be divided into two sectors: the sector of firms and that of households. We shall disregard the sector of non-profit institutions (although at certain points we shall refer to its role).
6. As we said in the introduction to the study, we shall not treat foreign trade.
7. Production will be divided into two classes known from Marxian reproduction theory: Class I, production of producer's goods, and Class II, production of consumer's goods. We assume that the exclusive buyer of consumer goods is the households sector which buys every commodity for money. Thus we disregard consumption allotted in kind to the population. The sector of firms buys the producer's goods, both of Class I and Class II.

It can be proved that the observations following below would be true under less restrictive assumptions. However, we cannot relax the assumptions because of the restricted space available here.

In devising the model I have tried to make it as comprehensible as possible, and so I do not present the model in a mathematical, but rather in a "pictorial", form. We shall use a *hydraulic analogy:* the flow of products will be represented by the flow of a liquid, e.g. water, and their storing by the storing of a liquid. The analogy is not new. At the London School of Economics the *Phillips machine* was shown several decades ago. This was a physical analogue model, in which the interdependences of the stock and flow variables of Keynesian macroeconomy, were represented through real liquid flows.[14] Here we shall use diagrams to replace both the physical analogue model and the mathematical description of the processes.

RESERVOIR OF CLASS II

We shall begin the description of the system by presenting the second reservoir storing the output of Class II. (See Figure 1.) This is to be interpreted in such a way that all products of the firms in Class II flow in there after production but before being transferred to

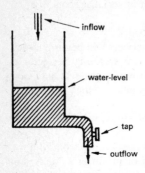

Figure 1: *The Class II reservoir*

households. It is as if, in accordance with our macroapproach, the total finished product inventories of consumer goods producing firms and the stocks accumulated in trade were collected into one huge store.

For the moment assume that the second reservoir is perfectly isolated from the reservoir of Class I.

What determines where the water level of the reservoir will be (i.e. of what size the stock of consumers' finished goods will be)? It depends obviously on the proportions of inflow and outflow. Let us consider as given the inflow rate or the quantity of products flowing in during a unit of time. In that case the water level depends on what outflow is allowed by the *tap* fixed on the reservoir. The tap can be regulated by changing the consumer price level and the nominal income of the household. Well-known elementary macroeconomic interdependences assert themselves here. The outflow grows wider if, at a given consumer price level, nominal income grows, or if at a given nominal income the consumer price level is reduced. In such cases the water level begins to sink, and if outflow is faster than inflow over a long period, the stock will be finally exhausted. From that time on only as many goods can reach the customer at every moment as have just been produced. And, conversely, the outflow will narrow down, if at a given consumer price level the nominal income of households goes down or, if at a given nominal income the consumer price level rises. The water level will rise in the reservoir, i.e. the stock of consumer goods will increase.

The tap can work because *the budget constraint of the household is hard.* The consumer can purchase only as much as his money allows (after deduction of intended savings).

Let us stop here for a moment, because we must talk about the importance of the water level of the reservoir. There is a close negative relationship—*ceteris paribus,* at a given organization of the system, and given adaptive properties of production and trade—between inventories on the one side, and intensity of shortage on the other side, or—in more general terms—between the slack in production and

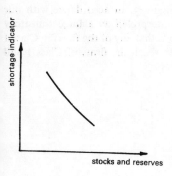

Figure 2: *Relationship between the intensity of the shortage and the quantity of stocks and reserves*

trade on the one hand, and shortage on the other hand. (This relationship is shown in Figure 2.) The relationship can be rigorously proved theoretically, and is also empirically verifiable. But now all we can do is to refer to intuition. Let us think of our everyday experience as buyers. If we set out on our purchasing route, and the shelves and stores of shops are full of goods, we can expect with high probability that we shall find what we want already at the first place, or at least after only a short search. If, however, shelves and stores are rather empty, it may easily happen that we shall be told not only at one but at several places that what we are looking for is an item in short supply. This is only a stochastic relationship. A larger stock cannot guarantee either the exact and immediate fulfilment of every purchasing intention, but it can reduce the probability of shortage phenomena appearing.

Given these assumptions, the consumer price level and nominal income (the "tap") regulate the volume of the inventories of consumer goods (the "water level"), and thereby the intensity of shortage on the consumer market.

RESERVOIR OF CLASS I

We present the first reservoir in Figure 3. In accordance with our macroapproach this can also be interpreted as a huge transitory store. Into it flow all producers' goods that any of the firms in Class I have produced; from there they can reach the firms of Class I and Class II that will use them for inputs.

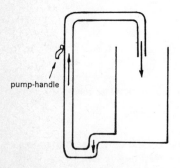

Figure 3: *The Class I reservoir*

As we have mentioned, it is assumed for the moment that this reservoir is perfectly isolated from the second reservoir.

In comparing the two reservoirs, it becomes apparent that there is no tap on the first reservoir. *The budget constraint of the sector of firms is soft.* Out of this reservoir the liquid flows freely: demand of the buyers (i.e. of firms in Class I and Class II) is not limited by their financial position. Moreover, it is not enough to emphasize that there is no tap. We can see *pumps* on the figure which pump the liquid out of the reservoir. The reservoir is empty: there are no inventories of producers' goods, and at the same time intensive shortage phenomena show in production. It is the first emptied reservoir that corresponds (at the macrolevel, and in the framework of the hydraulic analogy) to the system which we called "resource-constrained" in the first part of the study.

Before talking about pumps, we must make a remark. Let us not forget one important lesson of the microanalysis: shortage and slack are usually present simultaneously. Remaining within the hydraulic analogy we could say that the bottom of the reservoir is not entirely smooth. If we took a closer look at it (see Figure 4), we could see

Figure 4: *The residuum of surpluses*

that it is full of hollows in which liquid is held up. What is more, it is not water that is flowing in the reservoir, but a less fluid material which sticks on the walls and bottom of the reservoir. Turning now to economic reality: processes of the system take place with *frictions.* Adaptation goes on with delays and is accompanied by mistaken decisions. Therefore, *the siphoning-off effects notwithstanding, unsold stocks may decay and resources may rest unutilized.*

Yet now, for simplicity's sake, let us disregard consequences of frictions and revert to the rougher macropicture. We were saying that pumps siphon off more or less the reserves of the system; shortage is highly intensive.

FORCES OPERATING THE PUMP

Two of the driving forces operating the pump handles must be mentioned. *Quantity drive* in production may be induced by taut central plans. In this case firms are instructed to fulfil high production targets. It is well known that in the "classical" form of a socialist economy where firms received detailed instructions from the central authorities, managers were encouraged primarily to increase the volume of production. This phenomenon is, however, not necessarily tied to the system of instructions (which is only one of many possible types of signal from the centre to the firm). A similar effect may be asserted if the superior organ does not give instructions, but very emphatically declares its requests. Whether the form of signal from centre to firm is the former or the latter, tautness of the plan means, in any case, that somewhat more output is required from the firm than can be actually produced from the resources at the given organization and adaptive ability. Under such circumstances the phenomenon of "hitting the resource constraint", which we mentioned in the first part of the study, must come about.

It would not be correct, however, to trace back the quantity drive solely to the tautness of central plans. It may appear also if the central plan is more reasonable and moderate. *There exists also a decentralized, autonomous mechanism of shortage*. This has always added to the centrally generated shortage, and may become prevalent even if the central economic policy does not induce shortage (or only slightly induces shortage).

In this matter I recall the microanalysis in the first part of the study. As a consequence of the soft budget constraint the firm as a *buyer* raises an almost insatiable demand. Whatever the momentary supply of resources and inputs, the firm always feels that it is not enough. It is impatient; it urges the producer itself or asks for the intervention of superior organs.

And now let us think of the other role: the firm in its function as a *seller*. Really or symbolically, the buyers queue up before the firm; they are impatient, they press the firm. Even if it is not instructed to do so, the firm will start by its own will to hasten the drive for more production, so that it can satisfy impatient customers as soon as possible. For that, however, it needs more input itself, and this plunges us into the *self-generating vicious circle of shortage*.

Furthermore, chronic shortage, and constant hitting of resource constraints, i.e. physical bottlenecks, create uncertainty in the supply of materials. This generates a hoarding tendency. While output stocks shrink everywhere, each producer tries to pile up its own input stocks. Hoarding further amplifies the self-generation of shortage.

We can say therefore: *shortage breeds shortage*.

The other important driving force of pumping is the *expansion drive*. This may develop, similarly to the case of short-term decisions with current production, as a consequence of taut central investment plans. If economic policy wishes to extend production at a forced rate, it will usually determine ambitious investment targets with input requirements which exceed the available supply of investment goods. Investment actions keep hitting the physical resource constraints of investment.

Just as before, when talking about current production, we can establish here that the expansion drive does not need to be forced by central instructions upon the medium and low-level authorities of economic management and upon the firms. There is an *inner* force which promotes expansion drive. *Every firm without exception wants to grow,* and their "representative", the superior authorities, also wish the sector in their charge to grow. *Investment hunger* is general, and rises again and again, even if at some places it may be stilled momentarily[15].

There are a number of motivations for the inner expansion drive, and together with it, investment hunger. The most important of these is *identification* with the firm or in the case of a superior organ, with the sector under its control. Every leader is thoroughly convinced that the activity of the unit in his charge is socially important. He perceives that there is shortage in its output. Therefore, he considers expansion justified and urgent. We can see again the self-generating mechanism of shortage, but now in the sphere of long-term decision-making. The perception of shortage intensifies the expansion drive and investment hunger; expansion drive and investment hunger intensify shortage.

It is, however, not enough to recognize the positive motive that stimulates expansion and investment. It may be even more important to understand that, in the case of the soft budget constraint, *nothing keeps the firm from investment*. Investment risk has ceased; financial failure is impossible. There is no existing firm that would, once offered an investment opportunity, voluntarily turn it down. This is the most important difference between the two social situations with which we are now concerned, and which Keynes treated in his time. His problem was how the cautious investors, afraid of failure, could be encouraged, and in which way insufficient private investments could be completed, at least partly, by state investments. But we are faced with a firm whose "investment appetite" is unrestrainable.

A particular *investment money illusion* develops. It appears as if financial investment quotas were distributed by central organs: by the planning office, by financial authorities and by banks. In fact they allocate permission to start the physical actions of investment. And if action has begun, it cannot stop, not even if it costs much more money than has been planned. Money supply passively adjusts to the money demand generated by the physical inputs of the investment actions. The budget constraint of investment is also soft and ineffective.

Summarily, it can be stated that quantity drive creates an almost insatiable demand for inputs of current production, and expansion drive creates an almost insatiable demand for investment goods.

For a short detour I shall mention that the role of *non-profit institutions* is similar to that of firms from the point of view of processes examined here. They also know the symptoms of quantity and of expansion drive[16]. Thus they are also "pumping".

We have already touched upon the question of who in fact handles the pumps. If, as I have pointed out, it is the central economic policy that is at the head of quantity drive and forced-rate expansion, this fact reinforces greatly the effect of pumping. Yet even if central economic policy is more restrained, there are still hundreds of medium and low-level administrative authorities, and thousands of firms and of non-profit-making institutions who hold the pump in their hands. It is difficult to remind them of self-restraint. If anybody pumped less, others would pump away what he could have got. While not one manager of firm, non-profit institution or superior organ is pleased with the consequences of shortage, he still feels that he cannot stop, he feels compelled to pump.

LEAKS AND FILTRATION

The next step in our analysis is to do away with the assumption that the two reservoirs are perfectly isolated from each other. Let us have a look at Figure 5, which shows the two reservoirs side by side.

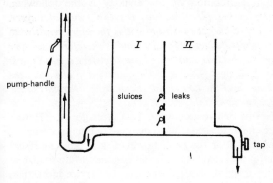

Figure 5: *Leakage*

There are *leaks* on their common sidewall, through which the liquid *filters*. Turning from the analogy to economic reality: there are no two separate markets hermetically closed from each other, one used exclusively by the households and the other used exclusively by the firms. These two types of buyers compete with each other for the same supply.[17]

Through the leak, water can flow in either direction, and this can in fact happen in the economy. (Private car owners buy up parts before firm-owned cars can get them, or the other way round.) Yet even if the possibility of symmetry exists, in practice the actual direction of the flow is usually asymmetrical: it is the sector of firms that effectuates *siphoning-off* for itself.

Let us not forget that there is a tap on the right-hand side, i.e. at the outlet of the second reservoir, while on the left side there is no tap. Let us assume that while the rate of flow into the second reservoir remains unchanged the outlet of the tap is narrowed (e.g. the consumer price level rises). For a time the water level will be rising. This will be, however, *ceteris paribus* only transitory. The law of communicating vessels asserts itself. If one vessel is full, while the other one is empty, and there is communication between them, the water level will even up. In the present case also, the level in the second reservoir sinks to the level of the first reservoir.

The economic interpretation of the analogy is the following. *Unequal competition takes place between the two types of buyers. "Household" has a hard budget constraint and is therefore sensitive to costs. "Firm" has a soft budget constraint, and is therefore hardly or not at all sensitive to costs. It sooner or later transfers a rise in cost onto the buyer or the budget. Hence, in the competition of buyers the firm has an advantage over the household; it can draw away part of the supply intended for the household.*

Let us examine one or two examples. Taxi fares go up. "Household" reacts to it as it has to according to manuals of microeconomics: its demand is reduced. For the firm, however, taxi fares represent a slight expense; if it uses taxis at all, it will continue to do so also at higher fares. What is more, it may even use the service more than before, since now it is more easily available, with less waiting time. Or let us examine a more serious example. Let us assume that the rents of publicly owned flats are drastically raised. This would induce a lot of families to voluntarily move into smaller and cheaper flats. If the rise in rents is high enough, there would even be empty flats after all the removals have taken place. These vacancies would be absorbed immediately by firms for the purpose of office rooms. The excess rent that would weigh heavily on the budget of the household would be easily paid by firms.

There are, however, several reasons why not all the inventories filter through from the second reservoir to the first reservoir according to the law of communicating vessels. We shall indicate only two factors here. One is "friction", which has been mentioned already. Purchase agents of firms do not pounce fast enough on goods; perhaps they do not need the concrete products that are offered to the consumer. The other reason would be that administrative sanctions forbid the firms to buy up products and services intended for households (e.g. it is forbidden to use rooms intended for flats for the purpose of office premises). It is such sanctions that are symbolized by the *sluices* closing or narrowing part of the leaks in Figure 5. Of course, it is difficult to enforce consistently such administrative constraints, and particularly difficult to extend them to cover all products and services ready to filter through.

Our conclusion is as follows: *shortage intensity on the consumer market does not depend solely on standard regulators such as supply of consumer goods, consumer price and nominal income. It depends also on the strength of the siphoning-off effect of the sector of firms or non-profit institutions.*

Emptying of the reservoirs, i.e. intensifying of shortage, occurs with particular force if, *ceteris paribus*, the tap of the second reservoir is opened wider (e.g. the rise in nominal income at given prices accelerates, and the growth of supply of consumer goods and services cannot keep pace). But reservoirs may also empty or sink to a very low level if that does not happen, and even with a restriction of household demand, given the assertion of the siphoning-off effect of the almost insatiable demand of firms not limited by budget constraint. This is the final reference to the hydraulic analogy. We can see, in a pictorial form, the flow system with its reservoirs, tap, pumps, leaks and sluices, which I called suction in my book *Anti-Equilibrium*.[18]

Shortage and inflation

In spite of the abstract character of our analysis, some practical economic policy conclusions may be drawn. Here are but two examples: the questions of inflation and employment.

INFLATION[19]

In Hungarian economic debates the idea has arisen that an effective antidote to shortage is inflation. At fixed prices shortage is intensive; at a rising price level this intensity would lessen. According to this, there is a "trade-off"[20] between shortage and inflation. The stronger the one, the weaker the other. The existence of a kind of "socialist

Phillips curve" is presumed. In my opinion this view is wrong. It is a view based on inaccurate assumptions which do not take into account the existing institutional conditions.

The trade-off "shortage-inflation" may in fact prevail in a *fully monetarized*[21] economy, in which the budget constraint for both household and firm is hard. In such an economy, if inflationary processes begin on the side of wages while the rise in prices is artificially restrained ("repressed inflation"), the expanding excess demand will obviously lead to an even more intensive shortage.[22] Under such conditions the release of the "repression" of inflation, i.e. opening the way to price increase, may drain the swollen excess demand. Demand constraint becomes effective again, and shortage may be more or less eliminated.

Yet all this does not hold for an economy which is only *half-monetarized*. In the institutional conditions that were discussed in the earlier part of the study, the sector held under the hard budget constraint is monetarized, while the sector under the soft budget constraint is only *seemingly monetarized*. *The sector functioning under a soft budget constraint does not react to price increase by reducing demand*. As I emphasized earlier, the firm is able to pass on any increase in prices of inputs sooner or later to the buyer or to the state budget. Therefore, its demand remains—also within any inflationary process—almost insatiable. What is more, this sector is able to engage in the siphoning-off process to the detriment of the sector that is yet held under a hard budget constraint, which would, in fact, react to a rise in prices by reducing demand.

As a consequence of the chain of cause and effect briefly summarized here, there is no trade-off between inflation and shortage. *Shortage is reproduced, at a stable as well as at a falling or rising price level, as long as the institutional conditions for its chronic reproduction exist*.

EMPLOYMENT

In a resource-constrained economy, after the transitory historical period of absorption of labour, full employment becomes permanent. This is one of the most important achievements of the socialist economy. At the same time chronic labour shortage appears as one of the manifestations of resource shortage.

Full employment is not brought about by specific economic policy measures aimed at increasing employment, and not even by planning or envisaging labour-absorbing input-output combinations. Explanation of the phenomenon must be found in the institutional conditions. It is a consequence of the soft budget constraint that demand for resources grows almost insatiably. Demand for resources, including demand for labour, necessarily has to grow as long as it does not hit the supply constraint.

This event appears in a "fixed package" accompanied by the other effects of a soft budget constraint: permanent full employment is concomitant with permanent labour shortage and other shortage phenomena. The reverse is also true: a genuine hard budget constraint usually keeps reproducing unemployment, together with the other negative and positive consequences of the hard budget constraint.

The great question arises: is it possible to develop a kind of in-between situation, i.e. a "convex combination" of the two different institutional set-ups and, together with it, such a situation in which there would be neither labour shortage nor unemployment? Or, do powerful social forces drive the economic system to either one or the other corner solution? The author has to confess that he does not know the answer to the question.

Finally, one more remark seems to be necessary. I have not made concrete proposals. I have not tried to elaborate a normative theory determining the method of overcoming shortage or the danger of inflation. I have strictly limited myself to the development of a *descriptive-explanatory theory*. The group of phenomena in question is extremely complex and complicated. Quite a few suggestions have already been made for solving the difficulties in the socialist economy with which we are faced here, but these have turned out one by one to provide only symptomatic treatment without eliminating the deeper-lying causes that reproduce chronic shortage. It is my conviction that efforts at a thorough analysis of the situation and at a better clarification of cause-effect relationships may promote the practical solution of problems.

NOTES

[1] *Real input*. The producer's material expenditures (raw materials, parts, machines and labour used) we call input and the goods or services delivered by the producer the output. The epithet "real" refers to the fact that "physical" inputs and outputs are being discussed rather than "informational" input and output.(*)

[2] *Linear programming* is a mathematical procedure for calculating an optimal plan of activities. One has to determine the maximum or minimum of the objective function under specific constraints. (For instance we must compute the firm's production programme that maximizes profit: here the objective function is the profit function of the company, and the constraints that no more machinery or labour can be employed to accomplish the programme than are currently available.) (*)

[3] See the section "Conflict between Expansion of Production and Production of Surplus-value" in *Capital* Vol. 3 [60]. The number in brackets denotes the number of the work in the list of references.

[4] See *Keynes's General Theory* [48].

[5] The idea arose already in the Soviet economic debates of the 1920s. In this study written in 1925, *Kritsman* draws the following comparison: "...in capitalist-commodita economy there shows a general excess, and in the proletarian-natural economy a general *shortage*." I found the quotation in *Szamuely* [77].

In his study written in 1970, *Kalecki* [46] stated it as an essential difference between capitalism and socialism that the utilization parameters of resources are determined with the former by the demand side, and with the latter by the supply side. Similar conclusions are reached by the Czechoslovak economists *Goldmann* and *Kouba* in their book [37].

[6] This is one (but not the only one) important way in which my train of thought on the shortage phenomena in the socialist economy deviates from the analysis that is provided by the so-called "disequilibrium theory". (See, e.g., *Barro–Grossman* [6] and *Portes–Winter* [70].)

[7] I intended only to give some hints of what the category of "shortage intensity" means. Because of limited space, we cannot go into further details of the problems of measurement in this study.

[8] This is expressed more fully in the next chapter.

[9] By this short description we wished to show that (a) the formation of expectations is based on the observation and subjective evaluation of the stochastic properties of recurrent events and (b) the degree of hardness and softness ought to be measured in fact on a continuous scale, since it is not only the two extreme cases that exist. It is only with a view to simplification of the exposition that my study used the dichotomy "hard" and "soft".

[10] The analysis for the time being is restricted exclusively to relations between firms and omits the demand of households and non-profit institutions.

[11] On Say's principle and Walras's law see *Arrow–Hahn* [5] and *Mátyás* [62]. Say's principle asserts that the decision-maker must not plan expenditures which are not covered by appropriate financial resources. Walras's law states that in a market economy the sum that those entering the market want to spend at given prices equals the sum that they wish to receive for the goods they are offering on the market. (The French Swiss economist Leon Walras put forward the bases of what is called general equilibrium theory in a book which came out in 1874.) (*)

[12] The detailed analysis of the capitalist system does not belong to the subject of the present study. I only call it to attention that also in modern capitalist economy signs of a slight (or not so slight) softening of the budget constraint are showing.

[13] The "stationary situation" is a phrase borrowed from the mathematical theory of dynamic systems. An economy is in a stationary situation if the essential characteristics of its situation do not vary with time; for example the same amount is produced and consumed day after day. In the vocabulary of Marxian theory of reproduction this is known as "simple reproduction". (*)

[14] The model was constructed as a visual aid by the same A. W. *Phillips* whose name became later known as a result of the "Phillips curve" describing the relationship between unemployment and inflation. While the Phillips machine demonstrates the flow of liquid under *pressure,* the present study is concerned with flow induced by *suction.* For explanation of the two expressions, see [52].

The idea of demonstrating interdependencies of shortage economy with the aid of a hydraulic analogy was inspired by J. Weibull.

[15] For the description of the regulation mechanism of investments, I made use of T. *Bauer's* research work [10].

[16] Here belongs the part of consumption that the population receives free, or almost free, at a nominal price (e.g. health service, education, etc.). These services reach the citizens through non-profit institutions. For a considerable part of them, demand is almost insatiable; intensive shortage phenomena appear. It is understandable that these non-profit institutions also take part in pumping.

[17] According to Figure 5 competition takes place for the products which the producers have already put into the "reservoir". In reality, of course, "competition" begins at earlier stages of the vertical process of production: which sector can suck up production inputs? This, however, cannot be discussed in the framework of the analogy that serves for a general framework of the macroanalysis expounded here.

In "filtration" an important role is played by foreign trade whose analysis is disregarded in this study.

[18] See [52, Chapters 17-22]. I have described here the same *phenomenon* as I did in the book, but *causal* analysis differs from the previous one at several important points. The explanatory factors that I considered the main cause of suction in *Anti-Equilibrium* played a role also in the present analysis, but only secondarily. "Weighting" of the causes has been rearranged. I consider now the *main* cause of suction the institutional background, concretely: softness of the budget constraint.

[19] To avoid misunderstanding let us establish beforehand the strong need to distinguish price and wage rises undertaken under a *once-and-for-all* price and wage reform from the *process* of inflation. The latter takes place amid lagged spill-over processes. Today's price and wage rises are the direct generators of tomorrow's price and wage rises, etc. The remainder of this study deals exclusively with the latter, the inflation *process*.

[20] *Trade-off*. Often there is a negative relationship between two economic magnitudes, so that the larger one is the smaller the other will be. In such cases one can talk of a "trade-off": reduction of the first economic quantity is "traded off" against growth in the other quantity, or vice versa.(*)

[21] *Monetarization*. Any sphere of the economy can be described as monetarized if the products or services pass from one hand to the other for money and if the price expressed in money of the goods and services has an effective influence on the buyer and seller. (*)

[22] For the theory of "repressed inflation" see *Hansen* [41], *Barro-Grossman* [6] and *Csikós-Nagy* [18].

"Hard" and "Soft" Budget Constraint*

The previous study touched on the problem of "soft" budget constraint. Let us now examine this phenomenon more closely.

The concept of "budget constraint" was introduced by the theory of household consumption[1] and then taken over by the general equilibrium theory. In this context, "budget" is of a general nature and serves to denote the plan for revenues and expenditure of any economic unit: household, enterprise or non-profit institution. It is thus not restricted exclusively to the fiscal plan of the central government. For those less familiar with the literature on microeconomics it will be useful to explain this notion with the aid of a highly simplified example and a related figure.

A factory plans a technological reconstruction, for which a specific sum, say 50 million forints, is available. It may choose at its discretion from various degrees of mechanization and automation. In the figure three *isoquant curves*[2] can be seen. Let us consider the lowest curve, T_1. Each point of the curve represents identical amounts of output: 1,000 tonnes a year. This amount can be produced by a number of combinations of "machinery" and "labour", using more labour and fewer machines or conversely less labour and more machines. The parallel curve T_2 above it represents a higher annual amount, 1,250 tonnes, while T_3 represents 1,500 tonnes, etc.

The two straight lines in the figure express two possibilities for spending the budget with two constellations of the price of "labour" and the price of "machines". The straight line with the lesser slope expresses that the firm may buy seven units of labour for 50 million forints if it spends nothing on machines, and three-and-a-half ma-

* First publication in English: " 'Hard' and 'Soft' Budget Constraint", Acta Oeconomica Vol. 25 (1980), pp. 231–245.

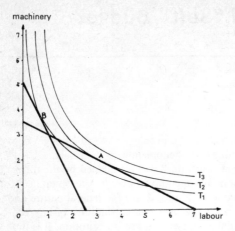

Figure 1: *Choice of the input combination and the budget constraint*

chines if it spends nothing on labour. Of course, every linear combination of the two kinds of input can be realized from the same amount. The steeper line presents the state in which labour has become expensive in relation to machinery. Now for the same 50 million forints only two-and-a-half units of labour can be used, but five units of machinery can be had.

From the firm's point of view the most favourable combination is provided by the point at which the straight budget line meets the highest isoquant curve. This machine-labour mix supplies the largest production from the amount of money available. With the less steeply sloping line (comparatively cheap labour) this is point A, and for the steeper line it is point B. With a constant budget constraint (of 50 million forints) the shift in prices has influenced the choice of technology: the factory opts for the reconstruction scheme that uses less labour and more machinery. This also exerts an influence on the surplus capacity that arises out of the investment: this cannot be 1,250 tonnes, only 1,000 tonnes.

However strong the simplifications may be, the figure expresses important relationships. In this model the decision-maker can only take into account alternatives which do not fall above the valid budget line. *Precisely on this account,* he is forced to react to prices directly. If the budget line shifts, he too *must* shift the point that represents the decision.

Anyone acquainted in another context with mathematical programming (e.g. applying a programming model to drawing up an investment or production plan for a firm) will obviously recognize that our figure presents a simple, two-variable decision problem. The budget constraint delimits the set of feasible decisions. The question we want to examine is the circumstances under which the constraint is *effective,* that is, when it really influences the firm's behaviour and under what conditions it becomes ineffective.

The relationship between the financial balance and the budget constraint

Let us now move from the schematic example somewhat nearer to economic reality. It will help clarification of the notions, if we leave open for the moment the question of whether it is a capitalist or a socialist firm we are dealing with. Later in the study *the historical realization* of the categories now to be clarified will be reviewed in terms of the socio-economic systems of various periods.

Everyone understands the concept of a *firm's balance sheet.* In its most comprehensive and general form it gives the following relationship as a summary reflection of financial processes in a period:

Terminal stock of money–terminal stock of debts $\equiv$
      $\equiv$ initial stock of money–initial stock of debts $+$
      $+$ credits raised during the period $+$
      $+$ other receipts during the period $-$
      $-$ credits repaid during the period $-$
      $-$ other outlays emerging during the period.

The left-hand and the right-hand sides of the balance are linked by the sign of identity. This identity between the two sides always holds tautologically. This balance cannot be "infringed upon". Even if the firm simply does not pay for the commodity delivered, the balance identity remains: one item in the credits raised during the year will then be the credit forcibly extorted by our firm from the supplier. This is why we say that the financial balance sheet, the *ex post* accounting of monetary sources and their uses is an "accounting identity."[3]

The financial balance may also be written in the form of an inequality. All expenditure may be put on on the left-hand side and all income on the right-hand side and it may be stated that expenditure must not exceed income. This is again an upper constraint of tautological nature, which is necessarily observed.

In the budget constraint the same items appear as in the financial balance sheet and in the constraint derived from it: money used for any purpose must not exceed financial resources. But the budget constraint is not an *ex post*, but an *ex ante* category. It is not "accounting identity," but a *behavioural regularity*. More exactly, it is a summary expression of a whole series of partial rules that jointly restrict the behaviour of the firm. To understand it, we must break it down into its components.

Hard budget constraint: the pure case

First we examine the *pure* case of a *hard* budget constraint. We shall indicate five conditions whose fulfilment guarantees hardness of the constraint. A theoretical construction is presented; one or another of the five conditions is never perfectly satisfied in reality. This will be explained later.

The five conditions together are *sufficient* to guarantee *perfect* hardness of the constraint. We do not claim that only this set of conditions can guarantee it. However, these five conditions provide a good starting-point for further steps in our reasoning. To facilitate subsequent comparisons we shall add the letter H(ard) to the serial numbers of the conditions.

Condition 1-H. Exogenous[4] prices. Purchase prices for inputs and selling prices for outputs are set exogenously for the firm. The firm is a price-taker and not a price-maker. From this point of view it does not matter who determines the price: an atomized market process that cannot be influenced by a single buyer or seller, a seller more powerful than our firm in fixing the purchase price, or a buyer more powerful in fixing the selling price, or a state price authority. It may be anybody. The main point remains that our firm is unable to influence the price.

Condition 2-H. The tax system is hard. This does not mean that taxes are high, but that the following principles are strictly observed:

(a) The formulation of tax rules (laws, regulations) cannot be influenced by our firm. They are set exogenously for it.

(b) The tax system links taxes to various objectively observable and measurable criteria.

(c) The firm cannot receive any individual, exceptional exemptions.

(d) The tax imposed is collected unconditionally on the prescribed terms.

Condition 3-H. No free state grants. The state does not give any grants to cover current expenses, nor does it make any free contributions to investment.

Condition 4-H. No credit. All inputs purchased must be paid for exclusively in cash. Interfirm credit cannot be taken up either by agreement with the seller or by breaking the contract, failing to make payments and thus forcing a creditor's role upon the seller. Nor can credit be obtained from any other source.

Condition 5-H. No external financial investment. Our argument does not cover the foundation of the firm, that is, the question of how the initial financial investment in the firm was made. We consider only existing firms. Condition 5 says: the owners can draw profit from the firm, but if they do so, they cannot reinvest it in the firm.[5]

Conditions 1-H,..., 5-H set *ex ante* behavioural constraints on the items on the firm's balance sheet. If these constraints are strictly observed, then the budget constraint summing up their effects does indeed restrict the freedom of choice of the firm, that is, it becomes a true constraint on *behaviour*.

Let us now examine the implications of these five conditions in detail.

How does hardness of the budget constraint manifest itself? (We shall again add the letter H to the serial numbers.)

Consequence (i-H): Survival. The firm's survival depends exclusively on the proceeds from sales and on the costs of inputs. If for a short time the latter exceed the former, the owners can avail themselves of the money reserves to cover the loss, and can renounce the withdrawal of profit. But if they fully renounced the withdrawal of profit and used up the reserves and the loss is still not eliminated, they are compelled to reduce expenditure. Less input leads to less output, proceeds will decrease, and finally the firm will become insolvent and go bankrupt. *The hard budget constraint is a form of economic coercion: proceeds from sales and cost of input are a question of life and death for the firm.*

Consequence (ii-H): Growth. Technical progress and growth of the firm, which require investment, depend on the same factors. *Financial resources to purchase additional input necessary for expansion of the firm are created exclusively by internal accumulation within the firm.*

Consequence (iii-H): Adjustment to prices. Prices being set exogenously, *the firm must adjust to prices.* Adjustment must basically be performed by *real* actions, principally by increasing or reducing the level of production, or by modification of the input-output combination. These changes are internal to the producing plant and are therefore not directly linked to prices. Indirectly, however, they are closely connected to them, through purchases of input which permit modifications in production and through sales of output made possible by modifications in production.

The firm may be helped in its adjustment by two *internal* financial variables: it may use its reserves and it may reduce or suspend the withdrawal of profit. The reserves, however, may be exhausted, and withdrawals of profit can only be reduced to zero. The firm cannot manœuvre by using *external* financial resources. Finally, therefore, no other means is left than to adjust through *real* actions.

Under such circumstances the price is not a mere "signal" which the firm can observe in controlling real actions or not as it feels like it. It *has to* observe it, because otherwise it will be incapable of development or expansion, and may even go bankrupt.

At this point we can entirely ignore the properties of prices. "Optimal", "non-optimal", "equilibrium" or "non-equilibrium" prices — it is all the same from the point of view of the *hardness* of the budget constraint. All that matters is that prices do not depend on the firm and that in the case of a hard constraint the firm *has to* adjust to them. (This is expressed in the figure by the shift of the decision from point A to point B under the impact of changes in price.)

Consequence (iv-H): Uncertainty. The firm does not share its risks. It bears the consequences of external circumstances as well as of its own actions.

Since prices are exogenous, they may bring disaster or good luck to the firm. In either case it will be the firm's own bad luck or good. If it is bad luck, nobody will help it out; if it is good luck, nobody will skim off the proceeds.

Consequence (v-H): Demand of the firm. The consequences enumerated above together imply that the firm's *demand for input is finite.* It depends closely on the purchase price of input and on the current and expected income of the firm, on its sales receipts. (In the figure, the finite nature of demand was expressed by the fact that only points on or below the budget line were attainable. The firm can buy only as much "machinery" and "labour" as its budget constraint allows.)

Almost-hard budget constraints

In every actual economic system there are several phenomena at work which shift the budget constraint away from the pure case of perfect hardness as described above. We shall examine below under what conditions the budget constraint should be at least *almost hard,* i.e. approximately hard. This will be indicated by the *consequences.* A budget constraint is almost hard if it causes the consequences (i-H/–/v-H) of the preceding section. Again we shall be content to give a set of *sufficient* conditions; there may be other sets of conditions able to cause consequences (i-H/–/v-H). (The letters AH following the serial numbers of the conditions indicate the qualification "almost hard".)

Condition 1-AH: Price-making within narrow limits. Some of the firms are *price-makers* for some input and output. However, in deciding on prices they are constrained by the resistance of their trading partners, and ultimately by the level of total demand.

Conditions 2-AH and 3-AH: No state redistribution among firms. Here conditions 2-H and 3-H in the pure case must fully stand. The state cannot redistribute the financial receipts of firms either by differentiating taxes and other methods of skimming off profits, or by subsidies and other grants.[6]

Condition 4-AH: Credit on hard conditions. This does not mean that the creditor demands high interest, but that certain principles—which are "orthodox" and "conservative"—are employed in granting credit:

The creditor (bank, etc.) grants credit to a firm only if it is creditworthy, i.e. it is fully guaranteed that the firm is able to repay it from the proceeds of its sales of output. That is, credit is an "advance payment".

If the firm has taken a loan, it must always fulfil every obligation in the credit agreement: instalments must be paid on time, and interest must be added according to the agreement. The adherence to credit agreements is enforced with the full rigour of the law.

The buyer cannot force the seller to grant credit by failing to pay immediately—without preliminary agreement—for the goods delivered.

Condition 5-AH: External financial investment on hard conditions. The internal financial resources of the firm can be supplemented by monetary investment by the owners. This may only finance technical progress and expansion of the firm and must be reimbursed from increased proceeds. No external financial resource can be used to surmount short-run financial difficulties.

We wish to avoid repetition. Reconsideration of what we said in the preceding section can convince the reader that consequences (i-H/–/v-H) listed there will occur in this case too. It must be added, however, that they cannot be guaranteed as strictly as in the theoretically pure case. It is true that conditions 2–3 have not changed: the possibility of state redistribution is still excluded. Yet even so difficulties may arise with conditions 1, 4 and 5. They deal with phenomena about which a simple "yes or no" statement cannot be made. We cannot say, for example, that credit is exclusively given either on hard or on soft conditions. There are many intermediate degrees possible. The situation is the same with price-making or price-taking, and with the hardness or softness of external financing conditions.

Soft budget constraint: the pure case

Intermediate cases will be discussed later; at this point we shall omit them and discuss the other extreme.

When can one say that the budget constraint has become totally soft, that is it does not bind *ex ante* the freedom of choice of the firm? We shall go over the five conditions discussed above. (This time we shall put a letter S after the serial number.) In fact, a single condition — or perhaps even a single part of a condition — is sufficient to render the constraint soft, though usually several conditions apply simultaneously.

Condition 1-S: Price-making. The majority of firms are not price-takers but price-makers. Price is not exogenous for most firms.

Theoretically this could be the case on both sides of the market — in input prices as well as in output prices. In practice, however, it is usually the latter which soften the budget constraint. The firm is able to impose its own cost increases on the buyer. This may be because, in the case of free contract price, it is the seller who is stronger than the buyer. (For example, a large, monopolistic seller is faced with many scattered buyers, or a chronic shortage allowed to dictate the price.) Or the firm can influence a price that is formally determined by an administrative price authority, because it has a large influence over the authority's decision.

Continuous imposition of all costs on the buyer is made possible ultimately by the fact that total demand in money terms is not strictly limited, but adjusts more or less passively to the rising level of costs.

Condition 2-S: The tax system is soft. A few characteristic manifestations of this are the following:

(a) The formulation of tax rules has been influenced by the firm.

(b) The firm may be granted exemption or postponement as an individual favour.

(c) Taxes are not collected strictly.

Condition 3-S: Free state grants. The firm can receive these in various forms:

(a) Contributions to investment expenditure, without repayment obligations.

(b) Permanent subsidies paid constantly in compensation for a lasting loss or to encourage some activity over a long period.

(c) *Ad hoc,* non-recurrent subsidies to counterbalance an occasional loss or to encourage a special activity.

Condition 4-S: The credit system is soft. It does not follow "orthodox" or "conservative" principles.

The firm is granted credit even if there is no full guarantee of its ability to repay it according to schedule from its proceeds from sales. Credit is not strictly an "advance payment"; the granting of it is not closely related to expected production and sales.

The firm is permitted to fail to fulfil the repayment obligations it has undertaken in the credit agreement. Moreover the firm in the role of buyer of input is allowed arbitrarily to postpone payment without previous agreement with the seller.

Condition 5-S: External financial investment on soft conditions. In the case of a firm in state ownership this cannot be distinguished from condition 3-S, where there are free state grants. Phenomena of this kind may also be observed in private enterprise: owners invest money from their own resources in the firm not in order to develop and enlarge it but in order to help it out of its financial difficulties.[7]

We can now contrast the signs accompanying the phenomena and direct consequences of soft budget constraint with those of hard.

Consequence (i-S): Survival. Survival of the firm does not depend only on a permanent ability to cover the costs of its purchases of input from the proceeds of sales. Even if the former permanently exceed the latter, that may be counterbalanced by tax exemptions, state subsidies, soft credit, etc. The difference between the proceeds from production and the costs of production is *not a question of life and death.*

Consequence (ii-S): Growth. Technical progress and growth of the firm do not depend solely on the ability to raise the financial resources for investment from internal financial accumulation (whether from its money stock, i.e. from savings from previous profits, or from hard investment loans which have to be repaid later from its own receipts). The financial resources needed to buy additional input for development and expansion may be provided by the state in the form of free subsidies or soft investment credits.

Consequence (iii-S): Adjustment to prices. The firm is not compelled to adjust to prices under all circumstances, for one of two reasons:

Either the budget constraint has softened as a consequence of the above-mentioned condition 1-S, and the firm is not a price-taker but a price-maker. For example, let us take the case where it is able to influence the selling price of its own product. It need not take much notice of the relative prices of input. However much they change, it will be able to adjust the selling price of its own products to cover cost increases.

Or, even if this method does not operate and the firm is a price-taker, it still does not have to adjust to prices by altering its input-output combination. If it disregards prices and suffers losses as a consequence, these may be compensated for by remission of tax, state subsidy, postponement of credit repayment, extra credit granted under soft conditions, and so on.

The survival and growth of the firm do not depend on prices. The firm takes note of prices only if it feels like it. If it does not feel like it, it can still survive and even expand.

The firm may react to changes in prices in its *real actions,* by making a suitable change of its input-output combination. This changes the *real quantity* of input purchased as well as the real quantity of sales, and thereby affects the firm's financial situation. Yet the firm may equally well react in another way, by trying to influence purchase and sales *prices,* and the *financial variables* (tax, state subsidies, credit terms, etc.).

In the first case the firm reacts in the real sphere and in the second case in the control sphere. In the first case it acts in the *factory* and in the second in the *offices* of the ministry, tax authority or bank. In the first case the main element in the reaction is *production*—the adjustment of the input and output combination to the new situation. In the second the main elements are requests, complaints and bargaining—in other words, attempts to *manipulate* those on whom tax remissions, subsidies, soft credit, and so on depend.

Softening of the budget constraint does not exclude the first reaction, but it does not enforce it and at the same time it offers large scope and even temptations to the second kind of reaction.

Consequence (iv-S): Uncertainty. The firm does not bear the risk alone. They are shared with the state. If circumstances develop favourably, it cannot rely on being allowed to keep the additional profit. Probably it will be skimmed off. However, if it has bad luck or cannot adjust itself adequately to conditions, it will probably be able to shift the consequences onto somebody else—the buyer by a price increase, creditors and primarily the state.

The financial situation of the firm and its budget constraint suffer from a double uncertainty. One is the kind suffered by every firm (even those subject to hard budget constraint): prices and markets are uncertain. But uncertainty is also caused by the constant redistribution of the financial receipts of a firm, for it cannot then foresee exactly how much the state will take away from it or how much the state will provide.

Consequence (v-S): Demand of the firm. The consequences enumerated above mean that the *demand of the firm for input is almost insatiable.* It does not depend either on the purchasing price of input, or on the current and expected income of the firm. Sooner or later it can expect to be able to cover its costs on input and if its proceeds from sales of output are insufficient it will be able to cover costs from an external financial source.

Ultimately, a soft budget constraint fails to bind the firm in its actions to the realm of reality—production and trade. *Soft budget constraint—unlike hard—is unable to act as an effective behavioural constraint and exists only as an accounting relationship.*

Let us glance again at the figure. In the case of hard constraint, the budget line is impenetrable; it is as if it were of stone, but in the case of soft constraint, it can be easily expanded, as if it were of rubber. Therefore, it does not determine the place of points A or B. The decision-maker does *not* form the input-output combination by adjusting to prices.

Elementary events and general behaviour

In previous sections we have considered the factors that harden or soften the firm's budget constraint. These factors influence the life of the firm at the submicro-level, through millions of elementary events. Objective events take place which are subjectively *perceived* by decision-makers in the firm. The decision-makers are affected not only by their own experience, but also by their observation of other firms. Finally, all these experiences form *expectations*. The hardness or softness of the budget constraint reflects what the manager of the firm expects in the future. The more he expects that the existence and growth of the firm will depend *solely* on production costs and on proceeds from sales, the more he will respect the budget constraint, and therefore the harder that constraint will be. And the less he expects this to be so, the less seriously he will take the constraint and the softer it will become.

It follows, as we have noted earlier, that the constraint need not assume one of only two different values: *either* hard *or* soft. There are also intermediate stages, for two reasons. First, one or other decision-maker may himself expect an intermediate value. Secondly, the expectations of different decision-makers within the same system may vary, some expecting a harder budget constraint, others a softer one.

There are, however, tendencies that lead toward uniform and extreme expectations. If an event occurs frequently enough which gives the impression of a soft budget constraint, and if its frequency goes beyond some *critical value,* a climate of "public opinion" will develop that regards the constraint as soft.

The degree of hardness of the budget constraint is *observable and measurable*. Since it is a very complex group of phenomena, it cannot be described by a single cardinal indicator. It can only be measured ordinally,[8] by several indicators together.

By making observations over a longer period the *normal degree of hardness of the firm's budget constraint* within the system can be established for given social conditions.

Observations about capitalist and socialist economies

Up to this point in the present study we have discussed budget constraint in abstract terms. We wished to elaborate the *analytical tools* (concepts, relations of cause and effect, principles of observation and measurement, etc.) so as to be able to examine historically materialized, specific systems. Now, in possession of the analytical tools, we shall begin to tackle this task.

First of all we shall make a few remarks about the hardness of the firm's budget constraint in a *capitalist* economy. Differences between countries are considerable, but looking back over a long period, a common trend is evident.

The normal degree of hardness of the constraint seems to have shifted: *the trend is in the direction of softening.* Perfect hardness in its absolute purity may never have existed, even though the capitalist system came close to this abstract extreme point in the then leading countries in the nineteenth century. Bankruptcy was real bankruptcy; the firm that failed was not helped out by anyone and was crushed ruthlessly by more successful competitors. The receiver selling up the bankrupt businessman's personal belongings and the debtor's prison were symbols of the hard system of taxation and credit. With a few exceptions (the railways, shipping, insurance, a few big companies engaged in colonial trade) firms were not large; prices were in fact formed mainly by anonymous market processes and were thus provided exogenously for the firm.

Significant changes have taken place since the initial period of classical capitalism, and these are moving the budget constraint away from the point of "perfect hardness". Although they are well known, we shall briefly review them.

The economy is becoming highly concentrated; huge corporations are being founded. They are no longer price-takers, but price-makers. This is one of the basic factors from the point of view of softening the budget constraint. A large capitalist corporation is able to react to input price changes not by adapting its input-output combination, but by adjusting output prices to actual costs plus the expected mark-up. By its price-making power it can almost "automatically" guarantee its survival and self-perpetuation.

Historical experience draws the attention of society towards employment, and not only the attention of workers directly suffering from unemployment but also the attention of capitalists and other strata of society. Bankruptcy is not solely a problem for the capitalist owner, since it always affects employment. Workers in a factory that shuts down are dismissed. What is more, modern economics has shown, that there are multiplier and accelerator effects; every bankruptcy reduces aggregate demand, thereby endangering employment at other places as well. It is not only the owners who are involved, but trade unions as well, and almost the whole society presses the state to save the threatened firm: it should be given a tax allowance, subsidies and credit with governmental guarantees. Rescue action sometimes takes the form of nationalization.

Protectionist state intervention is growing in numerous fields. The state protects domestic companies left behind in international competition, if their performance either in exporting or in import substitution is weak. For various socio-political reasons it subsidizes unprofitable products and services.

The growth of a firm depends not only on its success in atomistic markets but also on its power: the pressure it can put on its business partners, the relations it has with banks and, last but not least, the extent to which it can influence state decisions, taxes, subsidies and government orders.

Principles of credit are softened: in the Keynesian spirit they deviate from "conservative" and "orthodox" principles. A budgetary deficit is deemed to be permissible and even desirable in certain conditions.

We repeat that all the above-mentioned phenomena are well known from Marxist literature as well as from works of non-Marxist economists.[9] Here we have collected them according to a single criterion: we wished to point out that these processes all contribute to the softening of the capitalist firm's budget constraint. Today's capitalist firm does not react to circumstances merely through *real* actions. The bigger and more powerful the firm, the better our observation applies. The firm can influence its life in numerous other ways: from pricemaking to "lobbying" the authorities.[10]

As regards the degree of hardness of the budget constraint of the capitalist firm, no general proposition can be made. The normal degree of hardness is different in each country, depending on the level of concentration, on the economic activity of the state and on other social factors. It also varies within one country; it is different for the powerful and the weak firm. There is a sphere in which it could be said that the budget constraint is still "almost-hard", and other spheres where it is "not very hard" or "rather soft"—although nowhere under capitalist conditions has the budget constraint reached full softness, with an automatic guarantee of the firm's survival.

It is not the task of the present article to analyse in more detail the position of the capitalist economy. We have gone into the question this far mainly to avoid distorted comparison. We may compare *theoretical* cases: the "pure hard", the "almost-hard" defined on the abstract level, and the "pure soft" constraint. Or we may compare one *real* system with another real system. And in this case we must compare the empirically observable behaviour of the modern capitalist firm with what we can also observe empirically about the socialist firm. In respect of the latter our main hypotheses are as follows:

1. In the traditional socialist economy (prior to the reform of economic control and management) the budget constraint of the firm is soft.

2. A partially decentralizing reform like the 1968 Hungarian reform shifted the normal degree of hardness of the firm's budget constraint — to some extent. The budget constraint of firms hardened a little, but only a little. At least until the end of 1979 it remained basically fairly soft.[11]

3. The budget constraint is not uniformly soft for every firm. It is relatively softer in the preferred industries and for the biggest companies.

It is not mere chance that I have called the above ideas "hypotheses" and not "statements", even though they are verified by a hundred kinds of experiences and many papers have been published in Hungarian economic journals which support them factually.[12] Further comprehensive empirical investigations are needed before the hypotheses may be considered fully proven.

The validity of hypothesis 2 was confined to the end of 1979, leaving open the question of the hardness of the budget constraint beginning with 1980. It is known that one of the basic ideas justifying the introduction of the control system of 1980 was to "harden" the financial and credit system and to strengthen the economic pressure on the firm. It would be too early to make any statement on the extent to which this has been realized. The normal degree of hardness or softness of the budget constraint cannot change from one month to the next. As we have emphasized, this is a rule of behaviour, and human behaviour is shaped by much experience, long observation and "ingrained habit". Executives will have to experience *over long years* repeatedly themselves or observe what is happening to their colleagues in order to understand that losses are a serious matter, that transgression of the budget constraint is impossible and that the life, death and growth of the firm depend on the financial position, and in order for the recognition to become deeply ingrained in their consciousness and govern their decisions almost unconsciously, as a "conditional reflex". Therefore, an opinion on the impact of the 1980 control system can be formulated in this respect only after two, three or five years.

Budget constraint and profit motive

In conclusion it may be stated that many more questions remain open than I have succeeded in answering. We have torn out merely a single link from the chain of causes and effects. Here we have not been able to discuss at length what factors really do explain the normal degree of hardness or softness of the budget constraint, and the direction of a possible change: whether it tends towards hardening or softening. And on the other hand we have not shown all the possible consequences of soft (or rather soft) budget constraint: how it affects the adaptability of the firm, its demand and supply, the equilibrium of the economy, the emergence of shortage, etc.

Instead of digressing onto all these problems at this place, I shall confine myself to a single remark. Those well versed in the literature on reforms of economic control systems will have noticed that we touched on several problems amply discussed in that literature. Yet the focus of the reform dispute in this connection was "profit-incentive", whereas in this article the focus is on "softness of the budget constraint". This would be not worth mentioning if it were just a terminological difference. In that case this article might be blamed for altering terminology unnecessarily.

Yet the issue here is not merely a change of words, but differences in the logic of the argument and in the order of importance of the explanatory factors. The fact that the owners, managers and workers of a firm are interested in increasing profits does not *in itself* determine their behaviour. When profit incentives are combined with a hard budget constraint, efforts are directed towards the line of real actions. Combining profit incentives with a soft budget constraint gives at

least an equal role to the manipulation of financial variables, price
increases, running after state donations, etc.

An important problem for the situation of a socialist firm is the pro
portion of a managing director's share in the profits in relation to his
salary. And there is also significance to be attached to the formula
on which profit shares are distributed among workers, or how welfare
funds or tax paid on profit are linked to profit. All this is important
but *not primarily* important. In the case of a hard budget constrain
the managing director would not be indifferent to profit even if his
personal share were zero in the short run—since he has identified
himself with the survival and expansion of the firm and his personal
career depends on the degree of success of the firm in his charge. We
are not seeking to change terminology but to draw attention to the
fact that the main question—both theoretically and in practical eco
nomic policy—is not the actual form of incentive, but the regulation
of the survival and growth of the firm, and linked to these phenomena
the relation between firm and state.

NOTES

[1] As far as I know, it was introduced by the Russian theoretical economist
Slutsky in his classical study on the household [73].

[2] *Isoquant* means equal quantity. (*)

[3] *Accounting identity* as a concept can be explained from examples. The in
come and expenditure of a company in a year are *not* the same. Income may
be more or less than expenditure. On the other hand the total financial re
sources available to the company in a given year (including any reduction
in cash in hand) must under all circumstances equal the total money used
for any purpose including any increase in cash in hand). *As a result of the
definitions* of the quantities featuring in this relationship equality must hold
and so one speaks of an identity. So long as the company keeps its accounts
straight (and correctly records income, expenditure and the initial and final
balance), this and other similar identities must occur. (*)

[4] *Exogenous* and endogenous quantities can only be distinguished relatively
and understood in relation to some *model* (i.e. some simplification of reality
abstracted for scientific purposes). Endogenous variables are decided by the
model itself and exogenous ones are fed into the model from without. (*)

[5] Conditions 4-H and 5-H give *abstract* conditions which can be interpreted
only for a stationary economy, that is for simple reproduction. It is necessary

to state them in order to define the *pure* case of hard budget constraint. We shall return later to the problem.

6 This condition only excludes redistribution of money incomes *among firms*. It is compatible with state redistribution of incomes among various groups in the population, with high taxes levied on some groups and with monetary supports given to others.

7 For example, when a family business is in difficulties, the owners may try to refloat it using their personal wealth. This is, of course, limited by the size of that wealth.

8 *Ordinal and cardinal* as concepts cannot be explained exactly here. Let us instead illustrate the difference with an example. The speed someone runs is a *cardinal* quantity: someone who runs 100 metres in 10 seconds really does run twice as fast as someone who takes 20 seconds. On the other hand the points given for competition figure skating are an *ordinal* quantity: the judges decide how to mark the competitor they are seeing by reference to others (in the same contest or seen on other occasions). The points provide an *order of ranking* among the competitors, but no one can say that the skater who receives 5.8 points is twice as good as one who receives 2.9 points. (*)

9 The historical importance of the concentration of capital was first stressed by Marx, and later it played an important role in the thought of Hilferding, Lenin and Luxemburg.

10 The price-making role played by the big firm was first stressed in the literature of imperfect competition; starting-points were works by Robinson and Chamberlin. The work of Galbraith on the relation between the contemporary capitalist corporation and the state raised great interest.

The theoretical starting-point for active government economic policy pursued in the interest of full employment is *Keynes*'s activity; related pro- and anti-Keynesian literature is plentiful. The neo-liberal school must be mentioned especially: *Hayek, Friedman* and their followers who, while feeling nostalgic about the classical free market period, point out sharply several aspects of the softening budget constraint.

11 This hypothesis is indirectly supported by the following comparison. First I quote from an article on Japan in an American weekly: "...the combination of slow economic growth, competition from abroad and the rapid appreciation of the yen has proved fatal to many companies ...Last year [1977], a record 18,000 companies went bankrupt... the transformation may be painful..." (*Nagorski* [64]). On the contrary, in Hungary, following the price explosion perhaps one or two firms were subjected to a procedure of financial rehabilitation.

12 We should like to stress from among them the following ones: *Csanádiné Demeter* [15], *Deák* ed. [21], *Deák* [20], *Faluvégi* [26], *Fenyővári* [28], *Szabó* [75], *Tallós* [79] and *Vincze* [83].

Degrees of Paternalism*

Introduction

My studies do not presume to provide a detailed analysis of the social relations and political and power structure of the socialist economies. Now we shall discuss only one aspect of the social framework—the relationship of the state and the firm—and again without claiming to be comprehensive. This topic was chosen for the study because it helps in understanding the problem of shortage.

We begin our argument with an analogy: we shall examine *the economic relationship between parent and child*. Five different "pure" cases will be distinguished.

Degree 4:[1] *Grants in kind—passive acceptance.* The new-born baby and the infant of a few months cannot express his needs in words. The parents give him food and clothing "in kind" and care for all his material needs.

Degree 3: Grants in kind—wishes actively expressed. The child still lives with the family which supplies him with everything "in kind". But he can now talk and express his own wishes. He receives a lot of things without making a request; sometimes he asks for something, sometimes he makes demands. It depends on the parents' nature whether they assert their will, or make a compromise with the child and grant him his wish. Genuine "bargaining" takes place between parents and child.

Degree 2: Financial allowance. The child has grown up and moved from home, but does not yet earn his living. For example, he becomes

* First publication in English: Economics of Shortage, *Amsterdam, North-Holland Publishing Co., 1980, pp. 561–569.*

a university student in another city than where his parents live. His living expenses are still paid by the parents, but now in the form of a certain sum of money on which he has to live. If he wants to spend more, he has to ask for more. Requests, demands, resistance, compromise and bargaining have not ceased, but only shifted to another plane: the subject of argument has become the size of the allowance.

Degree 1: Self-supporting—assisted. The child has grown up and earns his living. Basically he supports himself from his earnings. If he earns more money, he has more to spend. But his parents are still alive and are prepared to give him financial support if he gets into trouble and asks for help.

Degree 0: Self-supporting—left to himself. The one-time child has grown up, earns his living, and his parents are no longer alive. His financial position depends entirely on what he earns. If he gets into trouble, there is nobody to help him out financially. He must rely solely on himself.

The foregoing five types will be called below the *degrees of paternalism.* In reality, other types may occur, and the combination of pure types is also quite frequent. These five degrees will be sufficient to illustrate our train of thought.

The position of the firm in the socialist economy

Let us now leave analogy and turn our attention to the analysis of economic life. In our formula let us substitute the state for parents, and the micro-organization for the child—a firm, non-profit institution or household.[2] *The degree of paternalism[3] in the relation between state and micro-organization is an important characteristic of the nature of a system.*

The economic interpretation of the degrees of paternalism will be demonstrated with a concrete example, that of the firm in the socialist economy.[4] Our main assertions are summarized in *Table 1.* The rows illustrate the five degrees of paternalism. There are two pairs of columns. One shows how the firm gets inputs wanted for current production, and the other one shows how it gets investment goods. Within each pair the left-hand column represents the situation under the traditional system of economic management prior to the reform, and the column on the right represents the post-reform state. By filling

TABLE 1

THE RELATIONSHIP BETWEEN STATE AND FIRM IN A SOCIALIST ECONOMY

Degree of paternalism	Input supply to current production		Allocation of investments	
	Prior to reform	After the reform	Prior to reform	After the reform
4. Grants in kind – passive acceptance	+		+	
3. Grants in kind – wishes actively expressed	++		++	
2. Financial allowance				++
1. Self-supporting – assisted		++		++
0. Self-supporting – left to itself				

in the latter columns we can see the conditions that have developed since the 1968 Hungarian reform. In the table, the sign + indicates that the degree of paternalism in question *applies for* allocating[5] the input in question, and the sign ++ indicates that this is the *predominant* or typical degree. Let us now examine the table row by row.

Degree 4: Grants in kind—passive acceptance and Degree 3: Grants in kind—wishes actively expressed. In both degrees the central authorities allocate inputs among firms in kind and by a rationing scheme without any substantial intermediary role for money. Degree 4 is the most extreme case: this represents central dictation, with no questioning of the users or serious consideration of their opinions. In the period of operation of the traditional system of management this degree appeared with varying frequency, in every historical period, and in each country and sector. The degree most typical of the tradi-

:ional period, however, is Degree 3, for the allocation of both current nputs and of investment goods. The central authority makes the decision, but in doing so it takes into consideration the wishes of the firm concerned. If the firm is dissatisfied with the allocation, it will ask for more, perhaps presenting an arbitrary demand or "lobbying" in order to have its wish fulfilled. The phenomenon of "plane bargaining" is well known in this form of economic management. The central authority wishes more output from the firm for fewer inputs. This is the issue over which bargaining takes place.

Degree 2: Financial allowance.[6] This comes to play an important role in the firm sector only after the reform, and in the allocation of investment. Such a relation develops between state and firm in the case when the investment project takes place within the firm and may even be initiated by the firm, but it is financed exclusively from the state's central resources. The investing firm wants more money while the decision-making authorities either refuse the firm's request or accede to it.

Degree 1: Self-supporting—assisted. This is the most widespread form in the post-reform situation.[7] Current inputs are allocated entirely or almost entirely on this basis. In accordance with the generally declared principle the firm is a unit with "independent accounting". It is obliged to cover its expenses from the revenue from its own output. It lives on its own earnings. Yet if financial difficulties arise, the state will help it out of the trouble by one of many kinds of financial support. We discussed this phenomenon in detail when analysing the hardness or softness of the budget constraint in the previous two studies.

The situation is similar with investments financed from the firm's own financial resources.[8] The firm is able to cover the costs by its own earnings. Yet if financial difficulties arise (for example, if planned costs are exceeded), the state will help the firm out. It will ensure that the investment project is not prevented by difficulties in financing.

In Hungarian economic life the practice has grown up that if financial difficulties arise at certain places in the economy—in certain sectors, in the manufacturing of certain products, or in foreign trade—the state will come to the rescue by taking over the burden in the state budget. This is a manifestation of Degree 1 paternalism.

Degree 0: Self-supporting—left to itself. This row is empty in the table. Neither before the reform, nor since its introduction has a situation occurred in which the firm has been left to itself in the real sense of the word, in circumstances where it might fail to overcome its difficulties.

Tendencies and counter-tendencies

The relation between the state and the micro-organization—that is the currently prevailing degree of paternalism—is an important element in social relations. Therefore, Table 1 has important lessons for the study of social structures.

Degree 0 of paternalism is the ideal of the *Friedman–Hayek* school. To tell the truth, this Degree 0 has never appeared with full consistency even with a capitalist system based on private property and independent micro-organizations. Mid-19th-century England may have been close to it, but contemporary capitalism has departed from it. The state intervenes into the economy in various forms. For example, in many cases it helps out in a paternalistic way firms which have incurred losses and are threatened with bankruptcy: by giving state guarantees, credits at favourable terms, tax allowances, and perhaps direct financial support as well. In periods of growing unemployment, trade unions also put pressure on governments to support firms in difficulties in the interests of maintaining employment. Friedmanites blame Keynesians for this increased power of the state which dampens competition and the "natural selection" that follows in its wake.[9] Keynesian ideas have obviously influenced economic policy-makers. It would be a mistake to believe, however, that a scientific trend of ideas could exert such a strong influence, unless the process of social development has prepared the ground and rendered politicians susceptible to Keynesian advice. Atomistic competiton with the micro-organization left entirely on its own has become impossible in our age, in which production has been enormously concentrated and state bureaucracy has increased and is becoming ever more powerful.[10] It would be absurd to expect that a government which relies on the support of the voters should tell the public that unemployment, the price level, economic growth, and so on, are all the internal affairs of the economy and that it, the government, takes no responsibility for them. The government *has to* assume responsibility for the economic situation—and its choice is only between different sets of targets and instruments for economic policy. It is therefore *inevitable that sooner or later more or less paternalistic relations develop between the firm and the state.*[11]

And, if that is the situation in modern capitalism, it must *a fortiori* be the same in the socialist system. The social ownership of the means of production is accompanied by an active role for state power in the economy. This activity may be limited or extensive, but it is always present. The central authorities take responsibilty for the economic situation and, at the same time, they want to use every instrument in the armoury which they deem useful.[12] A large and influential apparatus of multi-level control develops in the socialist economy which grows and becomes stronger according to its own laws. Its members identify themselves with their jobs and that gives them the drive actively to shape the course of economic life. All this explains why paternalistic tendencies appear "from above". These tendencies are complemented with demands for paternalism "from below".

Lower-level economic managers—the board of directors of firms, and their direct superiors—have ambivalent feelings towards paternalism: they both want it and protest against it. Let us first explain why they want it. *Paternalism means absolute protection and safety.* If a disaster strikes the firm, the state mitigates its effects or may even fully compensate for the loss. This is an extremely reassuring feeling. It does not only guarantee the mere survival of the firm but also ensures that it can even grow without its own financial resources, assuming that it has succeeded in acquiring the financial support of the state.

Let us turn to the opposite tendency. Several factors move the system away from the extreme degrees of paternalism. Here we stress only three of them.

One is the *demand of lower-level managers for independence.* We have just emphasized that their feelings are contradictory. While they gladly accept the safety provided by a paternalistic system, the other half of their soul grumbles that higher authorities are continually interfering with their affairs and are patronizing them. The knowledge that everything must be *asked for* creates a feeling of humiliation. They would like to rely on their own resources. This desire is one of the motivating forces behind reforms. It is this that drives the relationship between state and firm towards maturity or, in other words, towards lower degrees of paternalism.

Closely related to this is another factor working in the direction of reducing paternalism: *the frequent dissatisfaction of the public and of the higher leadership with the lack of initiative of lower-level managers.* Let us return for a moment to the analogy. It is known that the child who is overprotected by the parents will become passive and helpless. He will get used to decisions being taken and difficulties being overcome for him. The "educational effect" of the higher degrees of paternalism is the same in economic life. Passivity, complaints about difficulties, begging for the help of the state instead of coping with troubles on one's own initiative are all well-known and widespread phenomena. Recognition of the causes and consequences of these phenomena influence public opinion in favour of decentralizing reforms.

The two factors mentioned above are linked with the *behaviour* of economic managers. Let us mention a third factor, an *organizational* problem. As we have seen, in economic life the higher degrees of paternalism are associated with the use of the rationing scheme for allocation and distribution. Resources and products can be allocated through administrative rationing to firms, non-profit institutions and households only for as long as society remains relatively poor, and production and consumption are little differentiated. In such a situation allocation in kind is a relatively easy task. As production and consumption become increasingly differentiated, however, using the rationing scheme to distribute all inputs becomes increasingly difficult. *Sooner or later differentiation makes a significant decentralization of decision-making and of information necessary, leading to greater independence for micro-organizations.*

The effect of the factors working against extreme forms of paternalism is shown by the fact that—as it seems—Degree 4, the highest (grants in kind—passive acceptance), was not able to remain the dominant or general form of relationship between state and firm for an extended period.

Degree 3 (grants in kind—wishes actively expressed) has been the dominant form of relationship between the state and the firm for a long period. The reforms which started in the late fifties and early sixties tried to make further steps towards the lower degrees of paternalism. In Hungary, Degrees 2 and 1 have become dominant.

As was emphasized at the beginning of the present section, in this field there are strong tendencies operating in each direction. The course of history will show which tendency dominates in each socialist country, and how strongly it does so.

Paternalism and the softening of the budget constraint

Let us revert from historical prediction to present realities. According to Table 1, Degrees 1–3 of paternalism characterize socialist firms and, it can be added, the non-profit institutions as well. (Actual distribution may differ by country and by period.) And, if this is so, the question arises of how paternalism is related to shortage.

The most important link between the two sets of phenomena is the *soft budget constraint*. Degree 0 of paternalism implies that the budget constraint is perfectly hard. Whatever happens to the financial balance of the firm, the state does not intervene: it collects the taxes imposed by law and that is all. It does not feel "pity" for the firm, or help it out of trouble; if the firm goes bankrupt, that is its own business.

Degree 1 of paternalism means that if the firm is struck by financial difficulties, the state will help it out with tax allowances, credits at advantageous terms, financial grants, taking over the losses, or permitting price increases. It also helps a weak firm, or even a firm operating at a loss, to expand.

If paternalistic intervention occurs in one case in a hundred, the firm does not expect it. However, if such interventions are quite frequent, the firm's behavioural norms are established in expectation of it. This is exactly what we called the soft budget constraint in the previous study. *Paternalism is the direct explanation for the softening of the budget constraint.* And, if softening occurs, it will entail several phenomena connected with shortage: the almost-insatiable demand for materials and the tendency to hoard them, the almost-insatiable demand for labour and the tendency to hoard it, the almost-insatiable hunger for investment, and so on.

In the first study in this book we drew up the model of *suction* in which the "pumping" was done by firms and non-profit institutions. This is very closely connected with paternalism in two respects. One has just been explained: paternalism softens financial constraints on the firm's demand. (The tap does not work.) This is why the buyer firm pumps out as much as possible from firms selling inputs. Moreover, as we have repeatedly pointed out, a hierarchical multilevel system of control operates. Let us now consider not only Degree 1, but also Degrees 2 and 3 of paternalism. *Firms and non-profit institutions pump not only "horizontally" from other firms supplying them with inputs, but also "vertically" from their superior authorities.*[13] In the Hungarian language exactly this expression is used in the parent–child relation: the child "pumps" his parents. While he is small he asks for more chocolates and ice-cream, when he is bigger he asks for more pocket-money, and later still he will ask for larger family contributions to his first flat or first car. This "pumping" appears in the paternalistic relationship between the firm and its superior authority. If the superior allots materials and labour in kind (Degree 3), the firm or non-profit institution tries to pump out as much as possible. If money is granted (Degree 2), the firms and non-profit institutions strive to pump out the largest possible amount of money. "Pumping" may be done—as in the parent–child relationship—in many different ways: in a good case with convincing arguments, in a bad case with complaints or by "lobbying".

It can be seen from the preceding argument that *there is a close relationship between the set of economic phenomena in the strict sense (the soft budget constraint, almost-insatiable demand, horizontal and vertical "pumping") and the set of institutional phenomena (the higher degrees of paternalism): the latter set largely explains the former one.*

NOTES

[1] For the sake of the later reasoning it is advantageous to give the serial numbers in decreasing order.

[2] Like any other simile, this one should not be interpreted literally. Obvi-

ously, parents give their children the material goods which they have earned themselves, while the state carries out a redistribution. But we are not discussing here the origin of social wealth or the general theory of the state, but the limited topic of some features of the relationship between the state and the micro-organizations. Our understanding of these features may be helped by the analogy of the relationship between parent and child.

[3] The word "paternalism" appears in several works. See, for example, *Graaf* [38] and *Papandreou* [69]. We use the term in a special sense which is somewhat different from that of the works mentioned.

[4] For reasons of space, we shall not consider how the various degrees of paternalism appear in relationships between the state and non-profit institutions or households.

[5] *Allocative-distributive*. In economics the word allocation is used for allotting resources (such as labour or investment) between various possible uses. The word distribution denotes the allotting of income and property among individuals, social groups, strata, classes and economic functions. (*)

[6] This is the the the degree prevailing in the relationship between the central authorities and non-profit institutions.

[7] See *Bauer* [11] and *Falusné Szikra* [25].

[8] An important role is played by investment credits as well as by finance from the state budget and from the firm's own resources. Combined forms also exist. The various concrete forms of finance could be placed within a more disaggregated scheme broken down into more degrees of paternalism. Yet we content ourselves here with presenting the main outline.

[9] See, for example, Hayek's work in *Friedman–Hayek et al.* [29].

[10] This is suggestively described in an atricle by *Kaldor* [45]. He lays particular stress on the role of increasing returns in destroying the totally decentralized system, and on the growing activity of the state in securing growth.

[11] This phenomenon has long been known in Marxist literature; recently, however, other schools have begun to recognize it as well. *Galbraith* [36], for example, speaks of "bureaucratic symbiosis" in this connection.

[12] See *Tardos* [80].

[13] According to *Tardos* [80]: "...Firms frequently regard the state to be a milch cow, and the state—in spite of all promises of the authorities—can do little or nothing to overcome this attitude."

Economics and Psychology:
An Interview with János Kornai*

The buyer's and the seller's attitude

Question: *To which of the ideas raised in your book "Economics of Shortage" would you call the attention of psychologists?*

Answer: It would perhaps be better if a psychologist answered that question, after reading my book. I cannot help seeing things with an economist's eyes and cannot enter into the psychologist's ideas, examination methods or way of asking questions. However, I shall attempt to answer.

I would start with what is most closely connected with the subject of the book: how buyers and sellers of goods and services are affected by chronic shortage. In traditional economic theory the market is usually presented as the scene of equal exchange between buyer and seller. The buyer is willing to pay only as much for the goods as they are worth to him, and the seller will provide the goods only if he feels the price to be paid him is reasonable. That is to say, the relationship between them is based on equal terms. Although it may happen occasionally that one of the parties gets the worse of the bargain, this is balanced on average over a number of transactions. The market of a chronic shortage economy presents, however, quite a different picture: the buyer and seller are not equally strong. We say that a *sellers' market* is created. The sellers rule and the buyers are forced

* First publication in English: "Economics and Psychology: An Interview with János Kornai about his book 'Economics of Shortage'", Acta Oeconomica, *Vol. 26 (1981), pp. 389–402.*

The Hungarian periodical Pszichológia *published this interview with Professor János Kornai on some of the common problems of economics and psychology. On the part of the periodical, Tibor Engländer and László Halász took part in the conversation.*

to submit. Since the phenomenon is not individual or exceptional, but constant and massive, the *inequality of their positions* strongly marks the *attitude* of both the seller and the buyer.

Question: *At this point—talking about the attitude of the buyer and of the seller—your book uses a psychological category. What do you mean by it, in this context?*

Answer: I mean the *constant* disposition and behavioural pattern manifest in the formation of the seller's or the buyer's intentions, in their way of collecting information and in their decisions and actions. In a shortage economy the buyer feels himself defenceless and subordinated, while the seller develops a consciousness of power and dominance. (I would note here that by "buyer" I do not mean—here and in the following—just the housewife or other members of the household doing their shopping, but also the buyer for a firm or a non-profit institution, or an executive buying machines, ordering a building or taking acceptance of it, etc.). Well, the buyer—using the word in this wider sense—tries to be friendly to the seller. He makes efforts to win the latter's favours, so that he may be served instead of a competing buyer. This can take many different forms, for example, by reciprocating services, or even through bribery. The buyer tries to please the seller not only by what he gives him, but also by what is not demanded. He is humble and submissive, so as not to annoy the seller by expressing dissatisfaction, let alone by making any complaint. If the housewife quarrels with the butcher or even makes a note in the complaint book available in every state-owned or co-operative shop in Hungary, because the latter has cheated her over weight or price, she may achieve redress of her complaint. But in future the butcher can "punish" her: from now on he will give her less good meat; within the limits of legality he can put her in many different ways into a disadvantageous position. Something similar may happen in the relationship between a firm ordering the construction of a factory and the firm that contracts to do the work. If the investor is too demanding, the building contractor can retaliate in various ways: next time he will not accept the assignment or will put it further down on the list, etc. It is unnecessary to mention further examples, we are all closely acquainted with these phenomena.

Question: *How much, in your opinion, can these traits of the seller's and of the buyer's attitude be called general?*

Answer: They are certainly not the same everywhere, for they depend on the intensity of the shortage on the market of the goods or services in question. And of course they depend also on the personality, the individual character of the economic actor—the buyer or the seller. There are people who will now and then kick up a fuss, even though they have no hope of success. There are even people who habitually make protests and complaints. As for me, in my quality as economist investing the question, I do not analyse individual cases but a *mass phenomenon*—what is common to the many different individual attitudes. A certain situation—the power relation determined by the shortage economy between seller and buyer—will produce a certain type of attitude, formed by the role the individual will play in this situation. This is, by the way, clearly confirmed by the well-known fact that the same person who in his role as buyer will be submissive, in his other role, as seller, will be peremptory with his own buyers.

Question: *A psychologist would say that for the frustration suffered in his role as buyer he is compensated for to some extent by aggression in the role of seller. In this context the question arises as to how intensive frustration experiences are.*

Answer: I think that the intensity of such experiences shows a wide dispersion. There are petty annoyances—such as being unable to buy plugs or shoe-polish—which we soon forget. But there are experiences of shortage that affect one's whole life; let me mention young people who wait for years in vain to receive a council flat,[1] or who try to build one themselves, making huge sacrifices to do so. Or let us think of a patient who is defenceless through the lack of staff in the hospitals. It may not be a physical lack of goods or services that hurts, but the human experience connected with the shortage phenomenon: a rude tone, or a feeling that effort is useless. Moreover it is not only grievances that are involved, but a kind of permanent stress. Let us think of the foreman in the factory, the company buyer, the chief engineer and the managing director, who have to fight constantly for the acquisition of materials and parts, and in Hungary lately for labour as well. They live in a state of constant worry as to whether all the production factors will be available to them.

All that shows that the effect is quite deep, since it is wide-ranging and constantly recurring. But how deep is a question to be answered not by an economist but by a psychologist. The whole matter would be worth economists and psychologists investigating jointly.

I would, however, add that the problem is not one of full and total defencelessness and frustration, on the one hand, because although shortage is frequent with a lot of articles, it is not permanent or universal. On the other hand, the buyer affected by shortage can effectuate *forced adjustment* in various forms.

Question: *What do you mean by forced adjustment?*

Answer: The buyer, either the household or the firm in its role as buyer, would like to buy a particular article. Since he cannot get it, he buys something else instead. The substitute may be no more expensive but of poorer quality, or it may be of the same quality but more expensive. Thus the buyer is not left unsatisfied, yet because of his *forced adjustment*, he has suffered a loss. Another possibility: if he does not find the article required in the first shop, he will try other shops in the hope of finding it. Or he will postpone the purchase and try again later. The latter case may be connected with forced saving: the buyer does not spend the money he intended to spend, because he cannot find goods he would like, even by forced substitution. *Search, postponement and forced saving* are all further forms of enforced adjustment.

An important component in the buyer's attitude is the *propensity* to forced substitution, search and forced saving. It can be said again: this may vary, depending on the personality of the buyer. There are some who search and wait patiently; there are others who get fed up sooner and prefer forced substitution. As for the mass of buyers, however (on the market for a certain product or groups of products), buyers' attitudes show a more or less constant distribution of these.

The components in the buyer's attitude—let us now stick to this subject—are empirically observable and measurable magnitudes. They are parameters whose joint effect can be analysed theoretically as well, for example with the aid of a mathematical model.

What is expressed in the parameters of the propensity to forced adjustment is, in the last resort, that the buyer *adjusts himself* to the chronic shortage situation. We might say, these are the touchstone of the buyer's disposition to compromise and conform. There are many reasons why shortage becomes chronic. One important factor is certainly habit, resignation to the frequency of shortages and massive forced adjustment.

Question: *It seems that the various forms of forced adjustment are not found only in the economic sphere, but in other spheres of life as well.*

Answer: Development of the conceptual system and theoretical models concerned with enforced adjustment was suggested to me by experiences in our own life. However, I think that in the end we have arrived at categories suitable to describe not only the market of the shortage economy but numerous other phenomena as well.

To clarify what I have to say, let me draw a comparison with the traditional model of decision theory. This model assumes that the decision-maker has alternatives *at his disposal,* from which he can make a choice. He has only to consider which best satisfies his needs or what he has to give in exchange. Although it is now used as a *general* model of choice, the construction of the traditional model was originally inspired by the typical situation of the choice made on the free market. The buyer can make his choice as he pleases: he must only consider which goods best suit his taste and purse. On the supply side, alternatives are available to him without limits. In the course of a forced adjustment, the decision-maker undergoes a different kind of psychological experience: he is *deprived* of certain alternatives. Alternatives he knows *exist* and which others (or in the past, at more lucky times, he himself) have been able to get are now unavailable to him. He makes his choice with a feeling of deprivation and shortage. He cannot even think in terms of the "best". From the outset he looks for the "second-best". It is worth thinking about the number of situations of choice in which we make such forced adjustment. The search for "second-best" occurs in the choice of a school, a job, a partner in life, friends and company, and in political and social decisions.

The aspect presented here does not conflict logically with the traditional decision model. Instead it completes it. The latter considers what is *included* in the set of alternatives, while the former calls attention to what is *excluded* from it. The traditional model analyses the way in which the acceptance and effectuation of one alternative or another affects the decision-maker. The completion suggested enquires about the effect of the *lack* of one alternative or another on the decision-maker. Certainly, psychologists know a lot about this. They have studied the feeling of want. Certainly examination of the Hungarian socio-economic system could supply them with further data.

Question: *Forced adjustment, or the "second-best", does not necessarily entail the sensation of a loss. With the aid of processes of dissonance reduction, we may quickly explain to ourselves that what we have done is very good.*

Answer: This, however, does not change the basic consequences of the narrowing down of the alternatives, namely, the ingrained reaction that there are a lot of things in which you need not make a decision, because they have somehow been decided already. The choice has been made for you. Shortage keeps on making the *choice* instead of you. If there is only one course, you need not hesitate—and that is comfortable in a certain sense. The university student, for example, need not examine various schools and choose between them, for he only gets acquainted with one. The narrowing down of choice accustoms people to moving along the forced paths of a narrow range of scope.

Question: *Let us revert once more to the frustration caused by shortage. In your book you mention "tolerance limits". This is related to the category we call the "frustration threshold".*

Answer: I think it is, although there is an important difference. If I am right in saying so, the "frustration threshold" is interpreted in relation to the *individual*. We all "get upset" sometimes, for example, because of a distressing failure to buy something. My book, however, alludes to the *social* limits of tolerance. Of course, the limits of individual and social tolerance are correlated, but this correlation is rather complex. A number of important questions arise in this context. One sphere of questions is how frequent and how intensive the "upsets" are. Do they come in isolated instances and thus in the form of a lot of small "bursts", or do they interact and intensify one another in a chain reaction, leading to a major explosion? Do they only spoil the public mood, or do they also affect people's initiative and enthusiasm for work? The other sphere of questions is whether economic control and management bodies perceive that there are tolerance limits, and if so, whether they know where they are. Will they register small "bursts", or react only to the warning of an explosion that is already of societal dimensions? The traditions of his profession mean the economist deals a lot with *signal systems* and centres his research mostly on *price*, which is the most "economic" signal. It is emphasized in my book that in an economic system in which prices are not active enough as signals, a number of other signals function in their place. Grumbling, complaints and protests also serve as a signal system.

The role of tolerance limits can also be demonstrated by the development of investment in the socialist economy. Several scientists, among them Hungarian economists,[2] have studied the *cyclical* development of investment. I would stress just one point. The growth of investment sometimes accelerates markedly and that sooner or later impairs consumption. Living standards cease to rise or even fall, and supply gets worse. If that lasts a long time, public feeling may become increasingly tense. In such a case we can say the forcing of investment encounters the social tolerance limits of living standards, and a sudden slowing down of investment usually follows. First acceleration and then a sudden slowing down is what generates the cyclical movement.

The phrase "to encounter the social tolerance limits of living standards" indicates that control bodies perceive that the situation is stretched to breaking-point, and apply the brake straight away. But it may also happen that in fact the collision takes place first and investment is only slowed down afterwards.

It has always been clear to economists that economic growth has *physical* limits, imposed by available resources, and that there are also *financial* constraints. I wished to call attention, based upon Eastern European experience, to a further type of constraint: the tolerance limits imposed by the *mood of public acceptance in society*.

Behaviour and motivation of economic managers

Question: *Let us now turn to another psychological aspect of "Economics of Shortage", to the questions of the behaviour and motivation of the managers of the economy.*

Answer: A view held widely among economists is that managers are motivated primarily by their financial interests. Therefore their actions can easily be influenced by determining the economic indicators upon which their salaries and bonuses are to depend.

I do not in the least underestimate the effect of the direct material incentive. In my opinion, however, there exist some deeper-lying motives, which have a stronger and more lasting influence on management's behaviour. Of these I primarily stress that most people *identify themselves with their job* and feel its importance. If, moreover, a person is in a leading position, he identifies himself with the section in his charge. This applies to a foreman of the lowest grade as much as to the minister responsible for a whole sector of the economy. "I am the workshop, the factory, the sector"—the well-known phrase could be modernized in this way. This is one of the most important reasons, why the shop foreman or works manager—stimulated by bonuses—and the senior civil servant in a ministry, the minister, the hospital manager and the rector of a university—all on fixed incomes—behave in a very similar way in economic matters.

Question: *What does the similarity consist of?*

Answer: Of many things. We shall revert to some later on in this interview. For the time being, let us first look at a problem which I think is extremely important for understanding the functional regularities of a socialist economy, and that is the *expansion drive,* which strongly affects managers. This, in my experience, is to be found in every manager, both in those who have a financial interest in expanding the section in their charge and in those who have no direct financial interest. The manager of a firm would like to increase production through investment, but the minister would also like to increase the sector in his charge by means of investment, although his own salary will certainly not be the greater for it. The school head would like to have new or better equipment, more classrooms and a larger teaching staff. The general would like more arms and more modern ones, while those in charge of the protection of ancient monuments want more resources for that purpose, and so on.

Question: *It is conspicuous that this is called a "natural instinct" in "Economics of Shortage". Psychologists would doubt if this is really a natural instinct. In the animal world no expansion efforts are observed. Using an economist's expression, animals strive more after "simple reproduction", after their own and their species' preservation. Those living* *in herds strive to maintain the community and to preserve the area necessary for it, but they do not strive after unceasing expansion.*

Answer: It is indeed possible that in talking about a "natural" instinct, I used here a "colourful" expression which is not precise. The phenomenon meant is not a real natural instinct shared with the animal world, but a typically human inclination developed by social conditioning. I only wished to point out that it is not found only in one existing social system or another, but in the motivations of leaders of *every* modern, achievement-orientated society. It is an inclination to which the manager's function itself will inevitably lead. If what I have been saying about the manager's identification is true, if he has a feeling of "becoming one" with the section in his charge, it follows logically that he feels the activities of this section to be important. And if it is that important, it should also be enlarged: the hospital should be able to look after more patients, the university to educate more students and the factory to manufacture more products, and in each case with better and more up-to-date equipment.

To this is added the fact that even though such an expansion drive cannot be found in all men, it is precisely those who have it strongly that are most likely to be selected for leading positions: those with "drive", those who would like to have the largest possible unit under their control.

Question: *One form of identification is incorporation: you place the person or object (institution) in question inside you and make it one with you. It is interesting how much "infantilism" and "cannibalism" there is in this. "I like it so much I shall swallow it, or at least I clutch it strongly, lest someone take it from me."*

What you have outlined here refers at the same time to some kind of "latifundium experience". It is as if what happens in the manager were a feeling that the firm is his "latifundium". Permanent expansion is thus thoroughly understandable, since it is only the expansion of one's own organism.

Answer: The feeling of "incorporation" is found regularly. It is also expressed in the language used by the manager, when he talks in the first person singular, and says such things at a conference as "I shall produce those 10,000 tonnes."

Question: *If expansion drive among managers is that general, what is system-specific about it?*

Answer: The *inhibitions* that may, expansion drive notwithstanding, restrain the manager from making investment. I am not thinking of a case in which the state or the bank denies support or credit, so that the firm or the non-profit institution does not *get* the investment funds. The real question is, what inhibitions may lead to a situation in which, in certain cases, the manager *would not ask for credit* at all, and would show self-restraint.

I think that the use of the word "inhibition" is justified here. It is fear of financial failure that keeps the capitalist entrepreneur from easily deciding on investment. If the owner himself decides on investment, he knows that his own money is at stake. Or in case of a joint stock company, if the managers employed by the company make the decision, even though it may not be their own money at stake, a wrong decision will jeopardize their prestige in the trade and thereby their whole career. If prospects are uncertain, investment spirit will fade. This kind of inhibition is conditioned by social experience. Although not an everyday phenomenon, bankruptcy is not exceptional: in a number of advanced capitalist countries 2 to 6 per cent of enterprises go bankrupt every year. There is no absolute need to have experienced this yourself to develop this inhibition of prudence over investment. You do not need to have experienced a severe road accident yourself to be afraid of the fatal consequences of careless driving or of crossing the street without due caution. If sufficiently impressive, or let us say dramatic, indirect experience will be enough to develop the sense of danger.

And at this point let me pass onto what one finds in the Hungarian economy. *That kind* of inhibition has not developed in the Hungarian economy.

Question: *You cannot say, though, that a Hungarian manager, such as the managing director of a firm, has nothing to be afraid of.*

Answer: Of course he does. To mention just one fear, he has every reason to fear the disapproval and sanctions of the higher authorities. He certainly need not fear, however, that the firm will go bankrupt as a consequence of unprofitable investment. If the firm gets into financial difficulties, it will somehow be helped out of them. It will be allowed to raise its prices thus adjusting them to an unfavourable turn in costs, or it will be granted a subsidy, tax allowance, cheap credit, and so on.

Question: *In other words, the kind of failure the manager is not afraid of is exactly the one which is extremely important for appraising his performance.*

Answer: If I may say so, he will not hurt himself by falling. If he has mismanaged things, there will be no tragic consequences for him. He cannot come out very high, but he cannot fall very low, either. If all goes well, he will earn 15,000–18,000 forints a month instead of 10,000, he will get a state award and be interviewed on television two or three times. That is about the peak for the career of a company managing director. If, on the other hand, he commits stupidities, the only thing that may happen is that he will be transferred to another institution and another position, not much lower than the previous one.

Question: *So the two ends in the distribution of potential losses and gains are cut off, aren't they?*

Answer: That's right if one considers the gains and losses of a whole career. It can only move within a rather narrow zone, and within that zone it is not worth experimenting with too much.

All that leads to a situation in which investment hunger and the expansion drive are *unrestrained*. And since investment demand is almost limitless while available resources are limited, there is a constant tension in the investment sphere. The almost insatiable investment hunger "sucks" resources away from the economy. That is one basic reason for chronic shortage.

Reverting now to the psychological aspect of the question, an economic system is characterized not only by the motives of decision-makers for their actions, but also by the fears, anxieties and inhibitions that hold them back. I am rather inclined to say that the latter may be the more important and more characteristic. That again is a subject that would be worth economists, sociologists and psychologists examining jointly.

Question: *It seems that anxieties do not work either, when the investor submits his estimates of expected costs. He will always be underestimating them. Although he will cheat himself as well as others, his behaviour seems to suggest something else, to put it sharply, a lack of inhibition in asserting his interests. "In this way I shall certainly get the amount indispensable for a start and then come what may, we shall finish it somehow."*

Answer: I think that is a standard phenomenon, not only in the field of investment. It is worth anybody asking for something under-estimating inputs and overestimating outputs. That will certainly increase the objective chances (the money will in fact be given more easily), and at the same time be self-reassuring and self-encouraging. It is also remarkable that this is Janus-faced behaviour. If the one-time distributor becomes an applicant, the roles will change. As a distributor, he tries to press down demands, while as an applicant he will try to increase them.

This is a case of role-playing, and may also apply when someone building his own house asks for loans from relations and friends. Clearly it is no way of winning them over to say it will be eight years before the place is finished and that he will be obliged to ask them for large sums over and over again.

Question: *In addition to what has just been said, we should take into consideration a few other, generally characteristic features of information processing. In every uncertain situation we underestimate the total risk of the event, if the event is made up of a large number of details. We see the risk in perspective: the closer a partial event, the larger the risk will appear, and the more distant the partial event, the smaller the risk connected with it will seem.*

Answer: That is why in medium and long-range planning there is a common belief that the optimistic forecast will come true at the end of the plan period.

Question: *One may have serious difficulties now, but they will some-how dissipate by the time one finishes. But is irony in place here? After all, despite delay, a lot of pain and miscalculation, the output is there.*

Answer: True, but we cannot just accept it. The investment tension mentioned is one of the gravest consequences of it. And this not only has direct economic impacts—demand for machines, foreign exchange and building capacity will be always bigger than what is available—it also has disadvantageous psychological concomitants: haste and nervous tension. These will themselves generate confusion and work that run counter to the plans.

Question: *So far we have discussed subordination and domination in economic control and management. This must also have a psychological projection.*

Answer: Characteristic behavioural regularities develop in a hierarchical organization. Some of these are general, to be found in every hierarchical organization. Others are characteristic only of a particular existing hierarchy.

In Hungary, under the mechanism in effect before 1968, the upper level controlled the lower level principally by *instructions* (commands). This inevitably caused a "military" mentality to develop or at least acted in favour of such an attitude developing. The dominant leader needed to show a commander's virtues: an iron will, relentlessness on matters of discipline, a readiness to retaliate for opposition, etc. The most important virtue of the subordinate is obedience. A hierarchy based upon subordination and domination will not tolerate an individual raising objections, having a critical eye, or entertaining his own ideas. The two kinds of attitude are "compatible" within one personality: he will command "downwards", and obey "upwards".

So a mechanism built upon instructions has a far-reaching pedagogical and character-moulding effect. It will bring a rebellious person under this quasi-military discipline. As a matter of fact, the process starts earlier, with selection. A person able to command as well as obey has a greater chance of playing a leading part in economic management, and particularly of advancing faster within the hierarchy. One must add that this involves a group of socio-psychological phenomena which not only showed up in the framework of the old economic mechanism, but are present—frequently far more conspicuously still—in every hierarchy based on command and obedience, for instance in strongly centralized political or religious organizations.

Question: *From this point of view, what changes has the 1968 reform brought?*

Answer: The system of direct instructions has for the most part ceased, and so today the "military virtues" mentioned above are less sought after. According to its declared purpose, the reform ought to have led to a situation in which the managers of the producing firm display a far more "market-orientated" attitude: they should have enterprise, initiative and a commercial attitude of mind. Several elements of such behaviour have indeed appeared, but rather inconsistently, not in the last place because of the effects of the shortage economy referred to already. The "command–obedience" relationship has not disappeared, it has only been transferred in part into the relationship between buyer and seller. Moreover, subordination and domination have remained between the upper and lower levels of economic control, although its content, forms and "tone" have changed greatly. In Hungary today the higher authority does not issue commands, but recommends something or requests it emphatically.

Question: *In your book you use the word "paternalism" in this context. What does that entail and does it too have a psychological side?*

Answer: Higher authority may not give orders to the managing director of a firm, but it does patronize him. Like a parent unable to recognize that a child has grown up and continuing to interfere in his affairs—even though on occasion this may be in the latter's interest—the various higher authorities interfere in many different ways with the affairs of company managers. As with some young people, a great number of managers are unable really to grow up. The analogy well reflects in many points what one sees in the economy. The child of overbearing parents may protest against the frequent interventions, but gets used to them and in fact wants them. He will exploit the favourable sides of them: protection and security. If a managing director who has become used to paternalism gets into difficulties, if, for example, external conditions take a turn for the worse, he feels it is self-evident that he may appeal to higher authority for help. Since in most cases he gets it, a feeling of being fully protected is developed and he loses the habit of fighting against external difficulties on his own. Why should he, when there is a good father as a higher authority—the state that will always help him out of trouble. The representatives of that higher authority usually "grumble" on such occasions—just as overbearing parents do—that firms are unable to act independently. At the same time, however, I think the sense of being indispensable is reinforced: look, firms are independent, and yet they cannot do without us.

I hope that the rough outlines drawn here serve to make it clear that under the new economic mechanism in Hungary and together with it, under the new subordination and domination conditions where instructions are lacking, other kinds of human characteristics and behavioural patterns have become more conspicuous than the old ones. That is one more reason why one should not work with oversimplified models. Many different hierarchies exist. Each type of hierarchy has its own rules of the game that entail certain consequences both in selection and in shaping behaviour.

At this point we can take up again a thread dropped earlier: the question of material incentive. I have already stressed that the behaviour of managers with a direct material incentive and managers without one can be similar in many ways. Now I wish to repeat this statement in the context of all the phenomena that I have tried to present to show the behaviour of people within hierarchical organizations.

Let us take, for example, the old economic control and management system. The behaviour of the managing director of the firm was influenced by the bonus system, while his direct superior, the head of the industrial directorate, was paid no bonus. And the superior of the superior, the deputy minister, had no direct material incentive either. Notwithstanding, the connection between the managing director of the firm and the head of the industrial directorate (bonus "below", no bonus "above") was very similar to the connection between the head of the industrial directorate and the deputy minister (no bonus "below" or "above"). The *situation* itself, that is, any actual form of subordination or domination proves a stronger factor in developing attitude and moulding character at every level of the hierarchy than the special material incentive that may or may not be attached to it.

General methodological problems

Question: *During our conversation we have touched upon a number of overlapping questions of economics and psychology. How far are economists unanimous in their assessment of psychological matter?*

Answer: Not at all unanimous. Our discipline is divided into various trends or schools, just as psychology is. These schools do not usually state their standpoint from the psychological aspect, but one can demonstrate by adequate analysis, what psychological assumptions the theory entails.

I shall quote just one example: *neoclassical* theory. It is not exclusive but predominant in the West. The best and most thoroughly developed works of this school present the theory in an axiomatic form. They postulate in it as an axiom the existence of a *homo oeconomicus,* a rational decision-maker. The decision-maker "optimizes":

he chooses an action that will bring him maximum utility. This assumption is equivalent to the following: the decision-maker has a complete preference ordering over the set of alternatives. He is able to decide unambiguously in regard to any pair of alternatives which he prefers or whether he is indifferent to the choice. This preference ordering strictly satisfies a few postulates (transitivity,[3] etc.). This expresses ultimately that the decision-maker chooses consistently, that there is no contradiction between his various decisions.

The typical neoclassical commentary on this model is as follows: it is the utility function or its equivalent, the preference ordering, that is expressive of the "psyche" and „taste" of the decision-maker. To study how it comes about is not the economist's task but the psychologist's—the latter may co-operate with other disciplines. In any case, the preference order is "given" for the economist.

Question: *In your previous book, "Anti-Equilibrium", you polemized against the theory of preference ordering.*

Answer: Yes, I gave some detailed polemics there, but *Economics of Shortage* also touches upon the problem several times.

One objection is obvious, and has more than once been confirmed by modern psychology: a real person is not strictly and consistently rational, he is not *homo oeconomicus,* but a being full of inner conflicts and contradictions. Thus his actions are often inconsistent, and his preferences changeable and often improvised.

Another and far more important objection is that the model of a preference ordering is not productive enough. On hearing the objections, neoclassical economists are willing to expand the structure of the original model. For example, they suggest instead of a preference order constant in time, a preference order changing in time, or they postulate deterministically specified but stochastic preferences, and so on. Thus finally all kinds of human action are slotted into the model, but it has lost its explanatory power and become tautological. It says, "A person will always do what he thinks or feels is good for him. If he had not thought or felt like that, he would have acted otherwise." This is a truism but totally meaningless as a statement.

In my opinion emphasis in modelling the decision process must be laid on the *explanation* of the decision, on clarifying, *why* the decision-maker prefers one course to another. During our conversation, I have tried to clarify in connection with several subjects how the *permanent conditions* (social conditions, institutional framework, relative power position, function filled in the economy) of the economic actor can be used to explain the *permanent features of* the actor's *attitude*.

Economics is inclined to simplify the motivation background of economic behaviour: the capitalist owner maximizes profit, the manager of a socialist firm maximizes his bonus, the board of directors of an autonomous Yugoslav firm maximizes gross income, etc. This kind of description, I think, simplifies the description of motivation too much. There are many kinds of motives and they exert their effect jointly, sometimes conflicting with one another and causing conflict within the person who has to make a decision.

Question: *This corresponds to the psychological concept of "clusters of motives". It seems surprising to us that such questions are still disputed in economics. Another question arises in this context. In accordance with the theoretical standpoint explained above, in "Economics of Shortage", the word "optimum", much favoured by economists, is not used. On the other side, one often finds the word "normal", and the use of this word seems somewhat puzzling. The various schools of psychology and psychiatry are not unanimous in defining "normality", and doubts have arisen as to whether it can be defined at all.*

Answer: First of all I should like to clear up a misunderstanding. The concept of normality I use in my book has nothing to do with the psychopathological problem. For example, I speak about "normal queuing time". That does not mean that if someone is unwilling to accept this usual queuing time he is "not normal" in the everyday sense of the word and should be perhaps given treatment.

The concept of "normality" is used by several disciplines and not with identical interpretations. In looking for an analogy, my interpretation may be closest to that of physiology. Relying upon a large number of observations, the normal values for the variables of the human organism can be stated: the normal body temperature, the normal leucocyte and erythrocite counts, the normal blood pressure, etc. These normal values are *mean values,* and in a double sense: cross-sectionally (the mean of many men), and intertemporally (the mean over a long period). Some of the normal values are constant, while other ones depend on further variables (for example, age, body weight, etc.). As a rule, these normal values are not described by a single figure to several decimal points. They are quoted as a band, either narrow or wide. To each such normal value there belongs a *regulatory mechanism*. The actual value of a variable (such as body temperature or blood pressure) may fluctuate around its own norm and be affected by various factors. There exists, however, feedback regulation that will always drive the actual value back to the neighbourhood of the normal value.

That is the kind of concept of normality I use. It is therefore a descriptive category free from value judgement, which always points to the mean value of a variable. In my book I emphasize that one can speak about the norm or normal value of an economic variable only if there is a regulatory mechanism working in society to drive the variable deviating from the norm back to the neighbourhood of the norm.

It is in this sense, for example, that I consider shortage as a normal concomitant of a certain economic system and not as a deviation. And this implies that to queue up, to go in search of a missing article from one shop to the next, and so on, are part and parcel of the normal behaviour of a person living in a shortage economy.

Most norms are system-specific. In a given institutional framework given norms, that is, normal values of economic variables, will obtain. These play an important role in conditioning the behavioural patterns characteristic of the economic system in question, as well as in the constant reproduction of the important features of the system. Then at the beginning of a new era, a change in the institutional framework will sooner or later also change the normal values of the economic variables, that is, the norms of the economic attitude.

Question: *To conclude, one must not omit the usual question: what ought to be done, in your opinion, to bring about a closer link between economics and psychology?*

Answer: I should like to begin with a negative statement. I do not think that the usual forms such as founding a joint committee of economists and psychologists or signing contracts for joint research between economic and psychological institutes or departments would do. I do not really expect anything from reiterating empty phrases about "multidisciplinarity" either.

A few conversations between psychologists and economists, lectures held for the representatives of the other disciplines, or the reading of some of the important articles or books of the other might in a lucky case be very inspiring. For my part, I am grateful to several fellow scientists. At many points, sometimes in a flash, they have shown me connections that I could perhaps have understood less had I remained within my usual world of ideas, within my own discipline. I am sure that I and my fellow economists are open to the intellectual stimulation that comes to us from psychology.

NOTES

[1] State-owned housing in Hungary is allotted to claimants by town council or in Budapest by district councils.

[2] Of these particular mention can be made of *Bauer* [9], [10], *Bródy* [13], [14], *Lackó* [54] and *Soós* [74].

[3] *Axioms, transitivity.* A succession of scholars have worked out a rigorous mathematical model for what is known as utility theory (or preference theory). The theory considers the decision-maker "rational" and "consistent" if his decisions satisfy certain postulates. Of these one of the most important ones is the postulate of transitivity, which runs like this: If a decision-maker prefers Alternative A to Alternative B, and B is in turn preferred to C, then C cannot be preferred to A. The first two preferences are transferred to the relationship between A and C, and so A *must* be preferred to C. (*)

Comments on the Present State and the Prospects of the Hungarian Economic Reform*

1. Introduction

The mechanism of the Hungarian economy has gone through important changes in the last several decades, particularly since 1968. What we call a "reform" is a long historical process, that at times accelerates, at times decelerates, and in some periods even reverses itself. In recent years the reform process has again been advancing. It has already brought considerable results and its new upswing might greatly contribute to economic and social development.

The discussion is limited to the recent developments of 1979–82, and even these only partially, without a claim to completeness.[1]

The changes made in the period 1979–82 fall into three main groups, and this study divides up in a similar way.

Changes were made in the price system and in financial control (Section 2).

New opportunities opened up for creating small enterprises and expanding the non-state sphere (Sections 3 and 4).

The economic growth rate slowed down (Section 5).

The 6th and last section is concerned with the forces for and against the reform process.

* First publication in English: "Comments on the Present State and the Prospects of the Hungarian Economic Reform", Journal of Comparative Economics, Vol. 7 (1983), pp. 225–252.

2. The price system and financial control

We shall here concentrate on a few questions concerning the control of *state-owned large and medium enterprises* (for the sake of brevity simply "large enterprises" or "enterprises"). Some statements and some of the data in this section also cover, besides state-owned enterprises, the co-operatives, although the particular problems of the latter will be treated in later parts of the paper.

It was a repeatedly declared intention of the 1978–82 wave of the reform to "harden" the financial conditions of state-owned enterprises.[2] This phrase was used on more than one occasion in official pronouncements. The idea was that deductions from firms' profits and subsidies to firms had to be rendered "normative" (the term "normative" in Hungarian jargon referring to uniform, preregulated, deductions or subsidies that cannot be altered by bargaining). "Hardness" and the "objectiveness" of the management conditions were also designed to be furthered by the principles of the price system. Earlier the "cost-plus" principle in pricing had been applied: the price adapted passively to the costs even if the latter were high compared with world market prices due to low efficiency. Instead of this a price system had to emerge that adjusts Hungarian prices to the prices in foreign trade conducted in convertible currency. The intention was to stimulate enterprises to follow the signals of these prices, thus contributing to the improvement of the balance of payments in convertible currencies.

The efforts are remarkable in themselves, but the results have been rather mixed. Some of these intentions have been realized. The fact that the prices of raw materials, primary energy and many semi-finished products follow more closely than before the prices of imports from capitalist markets promotes rational calculation. The profitability of exports has become a much more prominent concern for enterprise executives. The other intentions have in our opinion been frustrated, or been realized only marginally or partly. I would like to emphasize three groups of phenomena.

Tendency of profitability to revert to the pre-1979 situation. A section of the Ministry of Finance[3] has examined the impact of the price revision on the profitability of industrial economic units (state-owned enterprises and co-operatives). They established what the profitability of the economic unit would have been if they had computed the actual receipts and inputs of 1979 not at the then valid old prices, but at the new prices valid from 1980 on. The confrontation of this profitability with the actual one in 1979 (i.e. measured at the old prices) indicates the "pure" initial impact of the price revision, before the economic units and the central organs could have adjusted to the new prices. This was then compared to the actual profitability. The latter comparison indicates the continuous impact of the price revision, including the adjustment of output and input to the new prices. The main data are surveyed in Table 1.

TABLE 1

REVERSION OF PROFITABILITY TO PRE-1979 LEVEL

Initial impact of price revision: Computed profitability in 1979 relative to the actual profitability of 1979	Continuous impact of price revision: Actual profitability in 1981 relative to the computed profitability of 1979	Number of economic units	Note
Increase	Increase	79	Reversions
Increase	Decrease	92 ⎫	of prof-
		⎬971	itability
Decrease	Increase	879 ⎭	in 971
Decrease	Decrease	86	units, or 85.5% of total
Total		1,136	

Source: Mohos [63]

We witness a tendency to revert to previous profit rates. It was only in merely 15 per cent of the economic units that the initial impact of the price revision was followed by a continuous impact in the same direction: an increase in profitability by a further increase, a decrease in profitability by a further decrease. In the majority of cases an immediate reversal occurred towards restoring the old profitability proportions. The tendency towards reversal is also perceptible if the figures for 1981 are contrasted not with the calculated 1979 profit rates but the actual profit rates for 1980. Of the 1,136 units examined, 741 showed reversal.

There are other characteristic data that also show the same reversion tendency. At the old prices industry contributed 60 per cent of the total profit of all enterprises in 1979 (total economy, excluding agriculture and financial institutions = 100). When we compute the actual output and costs in 1979 at the new prices after the price revision, the share of industry fell drastically to 48 per cent. But the restoration of the ratios immediately started: in 1980 the share of industry had already risen to 54 per cent, and in spite of the profit-decreasing central measures taken at the end of the year, the share was 55 per cent in 1981.

It seems *there exist deeply ingrained tendencies for old profitability rates to be reestablished despite the efforts of the price setters*. A similar tendency also appeared after earlier price revisions. Various explanations might be given: (a) there is a wide range in the quality of enterprise management and in the ability to adjust. A well-managed enterprise may soon recover from the unfavourable consequences of the price revision, while badly managed ones soon lose the advantages obtained by windfall; (b) differences in the prestige of economic units and in their relations to the higher authorities may mean that a "well-in" enterprise soon regains its old position while a "badly-in" enterprise soon loses the new advantages; (c) there may be variations in the extent to which an economic unit can escape restrictions and control. (To this we shall return.) It will be worth further studies examining what role these or other kinds of lasting deviations play in the reversal tendency.

Consider the most frequent case in which price changes initially reduce the profitability of the economic unit, but then profitability starts to grow again. This is a reflection of two processes. The first we can welcome: the enterprise adversely affected by the price revision immediately starts to improve its efficiency, it adjusts well to the market situation, and its profitability improves *because of this*. The other process frustrates the most important goal of the price revision: *the price-formation principle of "cost-plus" again asserts itself and prices rise*. Economic units that are favourably positioned for this to occur are those for which—owing to various reasons—the price level of the goods produced generally increases, or are those that produce differentiated products and whose range of products is frequently changed. There are several indications that this second process is at work. It is worth noting that enterprises in this category (initial impact: reduction, continuous impact: growth) are frequently outside the scope of the competitive price system.

Unchanged dispersion of the profitability of enterprises. Genuine competition in the market leads to a great inequality and differentiation of enterprise profitabilities. The 1980 price revision aimed at attaining an overall similar effect; however, that does not seem to have happened. Two reports, made independently of each other and with different methods, agree that *the dispersion of profitabilities has not increased.* According to a report of the Ministry of Finance the coefficient of variation of profitability of 1,163 enterprises was 79.4 per cent in 1979, while in 1981 it was 79.6 per cent for 1,168 enterprises — that is, it practically did not change at all.

Diverging tendencies in the profitability of exports and of domestic sales. An important goal of the 1980 price revision was to establish a connection by legal regulations between the profitability of domestic sales and that of export sales.[4] Thus, it was prescribed, among other things, that if the profitability of exports declined, the economic unit had to reduce the domestic price also, which usually entails diminishing domestic profitability.[5] It is difficult to check statistically in an unambiguous manner to what extent this principle has been implemented, particularly because of delays in adjustment. Therefore, we can draw only indirect conclusions. A Ministry of Finance study of 167 units drawn into the system of competitive prices concluded that the profitability of domestic sales was greater than that of sales for export. In quite a few cases the two kinds of profitabilities moved away from each other relative to the previous period: domestic profitabilities increased and export profitabilities diminished. It is not the purpose of this study to say if the firms concerned have infringed any regulations. Certainly this violates the *spirit* of the original idea. Several other observations testify as well that *in several cases the profitabilities of domestic and export sales continue to diverge from each other.*

We have surveyed three groups of phenomena to show that realization departed from intentions. When preparing this study, I first read the *preliminary* drafts and publications about the changes in regulators and about the price revision, and then the *subsequent* reports on the experiences. I saw a vision, as if I first entered a modern dispatcher room of a factory, with various "regulators": hundreds of buttons and switches, instruments and signal lamps. Dispatchers were bustling about, pressing now this button, turning now that lever. And then I got into the workshop, and I saw that materials were pushed about in wheelbarrows and that the foreman shouted himself hoarse. True, production is carried on, but quite independently of when which button is pushed in the impressive dispatcher room. No wonder, the dispatcher room and the workshop were not connected.

Of course, the picture is a caricature. But perhaps it makes clearer what *Antal* [2] called "regulation illusion". The regulations valid from 1980 on were worked out very carefully, with much intellectual input, to the tiniest details. But "those to be regulated" are moved by other forces (or moved *additionally* by other forces) and thus the actual events rather differ from what those working out the new rules expected.

What is the cause for the deviation between intentions and realization? The combined effect of a large number of factors, a complicated causal chain, asserts itself. We merely mention two interrelated causes.

One of those is the *artificial nature* of the system of rules and regulations. Real market competition is not devised by anybody: living organizations compete with each other for the buyer, ultimately for profit, for survival, and for growth. In our country, however, the intention is to simulate live competition with extremely complicated legal rules devised on a desk—with little success.

Let us return to one of the declared purposes of the price system: to prevent the assertion of the "cost-plus" principle. Practice again proves it is a *natural* effort of every producer who is not indifferent to profit that the price cover his costs and secure in addition a profit. The seller wants to get the highest possible price. There is only a single *countervailing power* to that: the buyer, who would like to pay the lowest possible price—assuming he is in a position to oppose the efforts of the seller to raise prices. The lowest price will emerge if there is competition among sellers for the buyers. For this, it is first of all necessary that the demand of each potential buyer (and thus also total demand) should be separately constrained, and that the ensemble of sellers should have some surplus supply, at least potentially, so that the buyer might choose from among the sellers. It might then indeed happen that the seller, in vain, wishes to get the price calculated according to the "cost-plus" principle—the buyer is not willing to give it, because he rather satisfies his demand from another seller (an immediate competitor or the producer of a substitute product). *The demand constraint cannot be replaced by an administrative or legal constraint on price.*

The price revision of 1980 sought through artificial instruments (legal rules) to induce producers and sellers to abandon their natural efforts and apply instead of the "cost-plus" principle various other pricing principles. In reality, the efforts of producers and sellers were directed toward the evasion of these artificial rules.[6] *The horizontal relationship between sellers and buyers, their conflicts and compromises, cannot be replaced by the vertical relationship between sellers and the price office.*

On top of the examples already given, it is worth recalling here the story of the regulations. It soon turned out that the prescriptions for price calculation were exerting a detrimental influence on efforts to raise the volume of exports. Enterprises seeking to raise domestic prices were induced to concentrate on exports of the most profitable products even if that export was relatively small. New rules were issued that allowed exceptions from the original rules. Thus, enterprises may now increase the domestic price of their product even if the profitability of exported goods does not improve, provided that the profits on export are at an acceptable level (for which exact numerical limits were prescribed) and the volume of exports increases. Several other —also concretely defined—exceptions exist.

Another complementary measure is that the enterprises operating in the non-competitive[7] sphere have to report to the Price Office if their profitability rises above 6 per cent (in the service sphere, above 9 per cent). In such cases the Price Office can forbid the further raising of prices, unless the part of the profit above 6 per cent is expected to be absorbed by rising costs. (This regulation was formulated from the outset so that it allowed for many exceptions from the obligation to report.) Beyond that, every economic unit has to submit detailed documentation to the Price Office every half year. The intention of all these measures is understandable: they seek to prevent "unfair profit". The consequence is that *the role of profits becomes illusory. In an attempt to improve the originally artificial system with ever newer corrections and exceptions, it becomes even more artificial.*

Another group of causes of the deviation between intention and realization is related to the alleged *hardness* of fiscal and credit policy towards enterprises. I have the impression that the words about "hard financial discipline" and "hard credit conditions" have not been sufficiently coupled with deeds.

The problem begins with the fact that *the new "rules" are, from the moment they are issued, custom-tailored to the special circumstances of enterprises.* In fact the contribution attaching to wages is the only deduction from firms' profits that is absolutely uniform. With all other forms the various sectors, industries and branches suffer varying treatment. The rules and prescriptions themselves have come to bear the mark of "peaceful coexistence" with the sector concerned and appreciation of its "special circumstances". This can be clearly seen in Table 2 which presents 1980 data. Column (I) shows the effect of

TABLE 2
COMPENSATING EFFECT OF TAXES AND SUBSIDIES ON PROFITS RESULTING FROM PRICE REVISION (1980)

Branch of economy	(I) Effect of price revision on profits	(II) Effect of tax and subsidy revision	(III) Compensation quotient	(IV) Overall effect of price tax and subsidy revision	(V) Note
Mining	+	—	0.91	+ ⎫	Taxes and subsidies
Chemical industry	—	+	0.90	— ⎱	virtually
Light industry	—	+	0.85	— ⎰	compensated for
Construction	—	+	0.82	— ⎭	effect of price revision
Metallurgy	—	+	13.77	+ ⎫	Overcompensated
Food industry	—	+	8.35	+ ⎭	for effect of price revision

Source: Communication by Piroska Horváth, Section for Financial Statistics, Central Statistical Office.

the price revision on profits. Column (II) shows the change in profits resulting from changes in taxes and subsidies: a plus (minus) sign indicates that profits rose (fell), and the net tax diminished (increased). In column (III) a "compensation quotient" is computed by dividing the numbers used to define column (II) by those used in column (I). This quotient is meaningful only for branches in which there are opposite signs in columns (I) and (II). Column (IV) summarizes the combined impact of the two, as it affects the profits of the industry in question.

Of course, this does not mean that the calibration of the price system and of financial supports and levies *ab ovo* compensated for every effect. Many enterprises fared well at first, others fared badly. But there remained sufficient possibility for manœuvring, and the course of affairs resembles repeated matches in a game. Both parties are masters in this *"regulator game"*; in addition they know each other's style well. One of the teams—the ensemble of the central organs—devises new tactics, new clever combinations, how to "get" the adversary. But the other team—the ensemble of enterprises—immediately works out countertactics and tries to get around the adversary. These countertactics have two stable elements.

One possibility which can always be tried is that *the enterprise does not implement the prescription*. Here the opportunities of enterprises vary by product group. If an enterprise produces only one or a few kinds of products whose quality can unambiguously be standardized, the price authority can strictly supervise it and check on the relationship between prices and costs. Such is the situation with primary energy, basic materials, simple standardizable intermediary products. But if the enterprise produces many differentiated products and sells them in several markets, then it is practically impossible to enforce the legal rules relating to price calculations. I had talks with experienced auditors and they acknowledged that an enterprise can evade the legal rules relating to calculations in such a way that it is impossible to prove that they have violated them. We have to put up with the fact that *it is the relatively smaller part of production where the method of price calculations can be prescribed in an administrative manner. With the greater part of production this is sheer illusion, only pseudo-administrative prices come about.* The 1980 price revision did not face this fact, and so quite a few of its prescriptions became illusory.[8]

The other possible defence tactic always worth a firm's trying is to *bargain*. We have already recalled the modifications made in several stages to the original principles for calculating prices. The regulations themselves provide scope for debate over whether the general system should apply to a particular activity or whether it should be qualified as an exception. And beyond that it is also possible to plead for individual, *ad hoc* exceptions. And so we are back with the so long familiar system of bargaining between central agency and firm. At most there has been some shift in respect of *who* it is worth bargaining with. Once upon a time the main bargaining partner was the ministry, later it was the financial authorities and the bank. Even today none of these have ceased to be possibilities, but now bargaining with the pricing authority promises to be the most fruitful. In this respect the 1980 reform has substantially altered the relative power relations between the state sub-centres: *the weight of the price authority, its power over the enterprises, has grown. But it is still true that the financial position of the enterprise depends not only on bargaining with its partner on the market, but also on bargaining with the state organs.*

A paradoxical situation has developed. The changes of 1979–82 promised an epoch of "hardness". The combined result of the changes was that too many enterprises got into a situation that, in the absence of a state subsidy, would lead to a catastrophe. If only a small part of enterprises were menaced, the state might perhaps have let things take their course, and these enterprises would have gone bankrupt. But what can be expected if many economic units, with quite a few very big ones among them, would stand at the brink of bankruptcy without support? The novel of Philip Roth, *Portnoy's Complaint,* described how its hero, when he was a small child, was punished. If the boy committed an offence, the mother, who otherwise pampered the child, chased him away with a slap on the back, saying he should now look after himself. He did that with great resolution at first, only to get scared after a few minutes and to ask to go back under the wings of the mother. "Hardness" and "becoming independent" merely strengthened in the child the feeling of total dependence and defencelessness, the need for parental care. The novel discusses at great length what a deep impression this feeling left in the soul of the overprotected child. The experience of the years 1979–82 left similar impressions in the "soul" of the enterprises: the promise of "hardness", and the very different implementation, a combination of "excessive hardness" and indulgence.

One of the important indicators of the financial dependence of enterprises on the state is *the magnitude of income redistribution among enterprises*. In one of our investigations[9] of balance-sheet data of state-owned enterprises we constructed an indicator of "pure", "original" profitability which was computed as if the state had not taxed away anything and had not given any subsidy either. A summary of the results of our research is given in Table 3.

TABLE 3

TAXES, SUBSIDIES AND PROFITS OF STATE ENTERPRISES

Year	Total subsidy per original profits	Total tax per original profits	Correlation between subsidy and original profitability	Correlation between total profit share going to employees and original profitability
1978	0.763	1.289	—0.66	0.03
1979	0.763	1.129	—0.59	0.07
1980	0.761	1.385	—0.59	0.12

Source: Computations of our research, cited in note 9.

As can be seen, 1980 did not bring any outstanding change. (In a more detailed breakdown—by branches or sub-branches—the proportions somewhat shifted, but this does not alter the aggregate picture of the whole economy.) Nor has the range of redistribution become smaller after the 1979 reform. Subsidy is still of a compensating or levelling nature; this is indicated by the fairly strong negative correlation between pure profitability and subsidies. Profits distributed to employees (as profit-sharing[10]) are almost *independent of the "true", "original" profitability of the enterprises*. We may add further that *the bonus of the manager of the enterprise also does not depend on the "original" profitability, but on the actual profitability after receipt of the subsidies*. The manager is thus forced not only by the interest of the enterprise, but by his own immediate financial interest, to acquire as much subsidy as possible.

The most convincing evidence of the "pseudo-hardness" of Hungarian economic policy is that while the Hungarian economy, similar to many other countries of the world, is in serious economic difficulty, and while the government is forced to carry on restrictive policies, *only one to two dozen firms show losses.* Out of 1,735 enterprises only 10 units showed a loss in 1980, and 11 in 1981. Only 13 enterprises were liquidated in 1980, and 11 were amalgamated with others. I took the data on enterprises incurring losses and on those liquidated from two different sources. I do not know whether the liquidated and merged enterprises incurred losses or not. But *Laki's* [55] data (1982) for an earlier period are available to answer this question. This excellent study performs many kinds of analyses, examining, e.g., the mergers in engineering between 1970 and 1979. In 27 out of 43 cases that could be evaluated in the three years prior to the merger, the profitability of the absorbing enterprise was lower than that of the absorbed one. Often in merger cases profitability diminishes and demand for subsidy grows.

One of the most important criteria of true decentralization is *whether difficulties on the national level are passed on to the enterprises so that they directly feel the national concerns. Our conclusions about losses, liquidation and merger of enterprises suggest that this has not yet happened.* Enduring losses do not lead to "death", to the liquidation of the enterprise; and conversely "death", the liquidation of the enterprise and its absorption into other units, may occur by administrative decision, independently of considerations of profitability. It is not the market that performs natural selection, it is the government office that orders decimation.

My book *Economics of Shortage* [51] concluded that the budget constraint for Hungarian state-owned enterprises has remained rather soft even after the 1968 reform.[11] From all that is said in Section 2 of this paper, the conclusion may be drawn that *the budget constraint of the state-owned large enterprise has not become considerably harder even after 1979.*

3. Concentration and deconcentration

The question of the liquidation or merger of enterprises leads on to our next theme: analysis according to concentration and size of firm. One new aspect of the 1979–82 period was that this subject came strongly to the forefront.

Let us look at the antecedents. *Hungarian production, particularly industry, is extremely concentrated.* This concentration was brought about continually over a long period, in both the state-owned and co-operative sectors. It is worth noting that a new wave of concentration broke in the years immediately before the 1968 reform: enterprise mergers, creation of monopolistic "national enterprises" and trusts, etc. Perhaps to those who were opposed to the idea of reform, concentration of production seemed a useful means of counteracting the decentralization of regulation. From Table 4 it is clear that

TABLE 4
CONCENTRATION OF INDUSTRY (1970)

	Share in the total number of workers (%)	
	Hungary	Sweden
Total industry		
Establishments with at most 100 workers	13.6	33.5
Establishments with at most 500 workers	39.8	67.5
Light industry		
Establishments with at most 100 workers	19.1	44.8
Establishments with at most 500 workers	51.3	86.0

Source: Révész [71]

Hungary's industry is far more concentrated than that of a far more industrially developed country like Sweden. Data for 1970 is given, measuring size of firm in terms of size of labour force.

In recent years the recognition has grown that the degree of concentration is too great. It is true that a giant company can progressively utilize the economies of scale in mass production, but on the other hand it is often more cumbersome and less flexible about adapting to swiftly changing circumstances. Let us look at Table 5, which groups firms by size of capital and gives profitability averages for each class of enterprise in 1980.

The data in the table are quite astonishing: *profitability decreases almost monotonously with increasing size of capital.* And let us add that the last classes, the largest ones, amount to 78.3 per cent of total net production.

I am not claiming that the profitability rating unanimously coincides with the efficiency rating. There are many different factors contributing to the higher profitability of the smaller firms: it is simpler to apply the "cost-plus" principle; they may be less burdened by international delivery obligations that are unfavourable from the

TABLE 5

SIZE OF ENTERPRISE AND PROFITABILITY (1980)

Value of capital plus annual wage bill (million forint)	Number of economic units	Average profitability (%)	Share in the net output of industry (%)
10.1–15.0	69	26.1	
15.1–30.0	232	21.3	
30.1–50.0	183	20.5	
50.1–100.0	219	19.7	
100.1–150.0	75	16.1	
150.1–300.0	121	16.6	
300.1–500.0	72	13.4	
500.1–700.0	61	11.1	
700.1–1,300.0	144	9.9	19.1
1,300.1 and more	131	6.9	59.2

Source: Communication by Piroska Horváth, Section for Financial Statistics, Central Statistical Office.

profit point of view, etc. But despite these reservations, the correlation shown in Table 5 deserves attention.

Háda–Trautmann's [39] article comes to a similar conclusion. They ranked industrial enterprises and co-operatives according to an index of economic efficiency. Of the first 500, none was among the 74 largest firms, of nos. 501–800, only 13 were, and all the others were among the economically less efficient group placed 801–1,156.

One facet of the reform process starting in 1979 is the intent to diminish the concentration of the state sector, in two ways. One way is *the breaking up of the huge existing organizations, to be initiated by high administrative decisions*. In January 1982 ten trusts and three large enterprises were split up to produce 137 independently constituted firms.

Another way of reducing concentration is *to found new small state-owned enterprises*. According to the new legal regulations of 1982, large state enterprises can found affiliates on their own initiative, and ministries and local councils may establish new small firms. Also so-called "small co-operatives" can be founded, and by summer 1983, 214 such had been created, with an average workforce of 50. Thus the small co-operatives as a whole now employ 10,000 people. There are fewer restrictions than for large enterprises. The central organs interfere less with the financial life of the small firm than with that of the large firm; they cannot issue instructions to small enterprises. The state has no authority either to regroup their assets. On the other hand small enterprises cannot expect financial support from the founding authority in the event that they incur losses.

Here we have again reached the problem we examined earlier in connection with the large state-owned enterprises: the hardness of the budget constraint. I do not wish to stop and assess the prior conception, because in the case of large state-owned enterprises enough emphasis was given in the prior declarations to the purpose of hardening the financial conditions. Instead it is more worthwhile examining the prospects of achieving those purposes. In my opinion, the hard budget constraint is more likely to be realized in the case of the small firms—although it is not quite certain even there. Let us consider only a single interrelation—that between losses and survival. The bankruptcy of a large state-owned enterprise might involve many thousands of people losing their accustomed workplace, which is a grave blow even if they can find new employment relatively quickly. Very strong prestige and power interests are attached to the survival of the large enterprise. This is why resistance to the hardening of the budget constraints of the large enterprise is so strong. In the case of a small firm, even if it is state-owned, that is perhaps simpler: both "birth" and "death" might occur in a more natural way. Precisely because the survival of the small firms depends on whether they can profitably compete in the market, these organizations will be prone to more rapid and flexible adjustment.

It would be too early to give a forecast for the number of affiliates, state-owned small enterprises and small co-operatives that can be expected to come about. The first central estimates are not very promising. For the time being there appears to be no vivid, spontaneous interest on the part of the ministries, local councils or large enterprises for the new possibilities. There arises another question: whether between the two extremes—the huge and the tiny enterprises—the medium zone is sufficiently represented. If the process proceeds at the conceived rate, it might take one or two decades until the size distribution of enterprises starts resembling the distribution established in the developed industrial nations.

4. The non-state sphere

In the official economics of the socialist countries the dominant idea was for a long time that the economic system would proceed towards an exclusively state-owned producing sector—a sector in "social ownership"—with large state-owned firms. Co-operative ownership was, according to this view, only a transitory form, even if the transition lasted for a long time. The reality of the socialist economy never conformed to this idea, and it is obvious that the Hungarian economy deviates much from it.

The present Hungarian economic system may be justly called a socialist-type "mixed economy" in the sense that it relies on the symbiosis of different kinds of ownership—and this entails a diversity of organizational and institutional forms. Besides the state sphere there exists—competing with it, complementing it and partly co-operating with it—an important, widespread non-state sphere. The measures of 1979–82 further strengthened the non-state sphere.

In the first place we summarize certain data on agriculture in

Table 6. Here the weight of the co-operative, household and auxiliary farms is the greatest and most conspicuous.[12] However, I should like to raise the problems of the non-state sphere in a broader way. We have a highly heterogeneous collection of activities and organi-

TABLE 6
SECTORAL CONTRIBUTION TO AGRICULTURAL PRODUCTION
(in percentage; all sectors together = 100%.)

State sector		Collective farms of co-operative sector	Co-operative farm members' household plots	Auxiliary and other farms
Crop farming				
1976	10.6	54.1	20.3	15.0
1977	10.5	52.9	20.3	16.3
1978	8.2	52.3	21.1	18.4
1979	8.8	51.6	21.0	18.6
1980	10.4	50.0	21.6	18.0
Livestock farming				
1976	5.8	16.5	38.3	39.4
1977	8.4	4.5	42.9	44.2
1978	9.6	16.6	43.9	29.9
1979	11.2	25.4	37.7	25.7
1980	11.6	24.7	36.5	27.2

Source: Central Statistical Office reports.

zations. Therefore in the following, we try to survey them according to several classifying principles.[13] The order has been determined not by importance but by the logic of the analysis.

1. SELF-SUFFICIENCY VERSUS ACTIVITY PERFORMED FOR OTHERS

For a long time and by many people the future of the socialist economy was thought to be such that activity within the household would become progressively narrower and a growing proportion of needs would be satisfied by various specialized large organizations (enterprises or public non-profit institutions).[14] Food would be supplied by large agricultural and food-processing establishments; people would live in rented apartments in large buildings; they would use mass transportation; children would be cared for in nurseries, kindergartens, schools and daytime homes; sick people would be nursed in hospitals, and so forth... This vision has proven to be extreme and one-sided. A considerable number of people want to satisfy a sizeable portion of their personal needs within the family, within the household, or on the basis of personal ownership and self-determination, either because of their own preferences, or because they are forced to by necessity caused by shortage.

Since the beginning of the reform process Hungary has made great changes in this direction although it is still far from satisfying demands, and from the full use of possibilities. I confine myself to only a few examples.

● This tendency is most apparent in *food supply*. Apart from their role as a producer of goods, household plots cover a substantial proportion of the food requirements of agricultural workers. Moreover, a substantial number of families of which the main wage-earner does not work in agriculture have an auxiliary farm or garden and keep stock, so that they are able to supply a proportion of their own requirements of meat, vegetables and fruit (and perhaps produce for the market as well).

● Private *housing construction* is widespread and increasing further. For this the family uses its own money and in some cases tools. In 1979, 42 per cent of all housing completed had been built by the population itself (with help, of course, from self-employed craftsmen or from "moonlighters").

● There has been a very swift growth that continues in the part privately owned cars play in *transport*. More than a third of journeys by individuals (measured in passenger/km) are undertaken in private cars.

● *Employment for women,* one of the big problems in Hungarian society, is closely linked with this problem sphere. During the period of swift, extensive economic development, women who had previously remained at home became one of the main new sources of labour, being progessively drawn into the corporate and administrative sectors. But the extent to which women were in employment then reached the socially acceptable upper limit. At the same time the question arose: who was going to fulfil the functions previously fulfilled by the women who stayed at home? Child-care institutions, hospitals, old people's homes, dry-cleaners, canteens and restaurants, cleaning companies and other service companies and institutions can only fulfil a proportion of them, looking at the matter solely from the point of view of service capacity. Moreover, in many cases the service provided by an organized institution is more expensive (certainly more capital intensive), less careful and of a lower standard than that the household could provide for itself. The problem has many ins and outs which there is no space to go into here (for instance the advantages and disadvantages of employment from the woman's point of view). All I have aimed to elucidate is that employment of women is an integral part of the more general "state-sphere, non-state sphere" problem. If to only a small extent, there has been a perceptible reversal of the old one-sided tendency. A significant proportion of women are happy to take advantage of child-care allowance,[15] and may break their employment relations for quite long periods to bring up their children. Many would prefer to work part-time if this were not impeded by various inflexible regulations. One secret behind the agricultural achievements is that women who stay in the household are supplying a significant proportion of the labour put into the household plots. Many in the towns, too, accept industrial or clerical tasks as outworkers so as to remain at home, keep an eye on the children and look after their people.

It is debatable how far Hungarian society can or wants to go in placing activities onto the shoulders of the family. What in this respect will be the demand from the general public? How does this relate to official economic and social policy, how much will it tolerate, how much will it restrict and combat it, and alternately, how much will it encourage and support it? In all events, this is one of the major factors deciding the size of the role in the life of the individuals and society that the "state sector", the large state-owned firms and the public authorities, will play.

2. FORMAL VERSUS INFORMAL SECTOR

A part of the activities performed "for others" takes place in the "formal sector" (by state enterprises and co-operatives, public non-profit-making institutions and by private artisans and private dealers who operate under official licence and under official control and pay taxes); another part takes place in the "informal sector". According to earlier concepts, in a socialist economy only the formal sector would be allowed to operate. In Hungary today the formal sector is dominating, but the informal sector is at the same time very large. Many people provide services for others—mainly for money, perhaps for other compensation—beyond the formal organization. A few characteristic fields are:

● *Material services,* e.g. repair, housework, construction, gardening, transportation of goods and people, etc. Income from informal "moonlighting" is earned by 150,000–200,000 people in housing and holiday-home construction, 100,000 in housing maintenance and another 100,000 in repair activities on clothing, ironwork, cars, telecommunications, etc.

● *Intellectual services,* e.g. medical treatment, legal counselling, engineering design, translation, typewriting, child-minding, etc. There are no estimates available on the volume of this kind of activity.

● *Housing services,* total or partial, long-range or temporary leasing of dwellings, homes, holiday homes. Around 200,000 families obtain extra income from this source.

An informal sector exists in every society. At a low level of development this is because the large formal organizations have not yet emerged, while at a higher level of capitalist development it is because a proportion of people attempt to escape at least partially from the authority and taxation of the state and the obligations and discipline of large organizations. This sector has always existed in Hungary. It has been characteristic of the last 10–15 years for it to broaden rapidly. In the strict sense of the term the informal sector performs a function of substituting for shortage; to a significant degree it meets the demand the formal sector is unable to satisfy.

The "informal sector" is a collective notion. It comprises activities that are illegal and persecuted, illegal and tacitly tolerated, and those which are not illegal and are carried out outside the formal organizations but approved of and patronized by the state. The objective of the new 1982 measures is to bring into the open the informal activities judged to be useful, to create for them a legal framework and—to a certain extent—to support their expansion.

3. FORMS OF OWNERSHIP

One of the most important questions is: who owns the means of production necessary for carrying out the economic activity? The three pure types are state, co-operative and private ownership. In the 1979–82 period there was an effort to remove obstacles impeding the development of co-operatives not only in agriculture, but in industry and construction as well. Similarly, the intention is also to allow the expansion of the "formal" handicrafts and small retailers, who work under official licences and pay regular taxes.

The various combinations of public (state or co-operative) and private ownership and of public and private activities now existing are surveyed in Table 7. The 1982 rules introduced a number of new forms (first of all the "economic working teams" in the second row of the table); but it also tried to expand the range of the old forms. Form 2 in Table 7 is a new experiment in channelling the widespread illegal Form 3 into a legal framework. It would be premature to discuss experiences with this.

A variety of ideas for further forms were put forward. One was for a mixed-ownership "joint-stock company" whose capital would be for a particular purpose such as housing construction, and be provided in part by the state and in part by private persons. Interest was aroused by the idea Tibor Liska put forward for making general a form similar to Form 1 in Table 7: units in state ownership would pass through auction into the hands of the entrepreneur who offered the highest rental. He would be free to do what he wanted with income exceeding rental, but the unit of proprietorship could be "auctioned away" from him, with suitable compensation being paid, if a new entrepreneur turned up promising more.[16] Practical trials of Liska's ideas have begun in certain places. Practice may also throw up further forms.

It is difficult to foretell whether the mixed forms of ownership will

TABLE 7

COMBINATIONS OF PUBLIC OWNERSHIP AND PRIVATE
ENTREPRENEURIAL ACTIVITIES

Form	Owner of the means of production	User of the means of production	Arrangement for use of capital equipment	Typical branches
1	State enterprise or co-operative	Private persons or group of private persons	Leasing fixed capital for a definite rent[a] In some cases the lessee is chosen through auction	Catering, trade
2	Partly state enterprise or public institution, partly the user	"Economic working team" formed from the employees	The team works under the protection of the employer, and uses part of the fixed assets for which it pays rent	Maintenance, repair, fitting (as yet preliminarily planned)
3	Partly state enterprise or public institution, partly the user	Workers of the enterprise or institution in question	Illegal informal work done during regular working hours, perhaps with use of employer's equipment	Construction, maintenance work, repairs, trucking

[a] A related form is the so-called "contractual" operation; in this form the owner enterprise or co-operative also procures a portion of the materials.

expand or contract. *There is enterprising spirit in several layers of the population. The question is whether this spirit will be supported or cooled down by the administrative, legal and economic measures.* I mention only the single example of shops and catering units offered for leasing and contractual operation. Till the end of 1981, from the 1,868 catering units offered, 1,184 (or 63.4 per cent) were actually rented or contracted out, and from the 1,630 shops, 461 (28.3 per cent); no leaser or contractual partner could be found for the rest. The main obstacle was said to be the high rent asked from the private entrepreneur. The experience of the next few years will tell whether the state organs, public institutions and public enterprises will show sufficient patience towards these "mixed forms", and whether the stability of their legal position, which is necessary for their taking roots, can be secured.

4. WORKTIME

The majority of those employed in the state sector work exclusively the legal hours. (Overtime does exist, but its volume is limited by strict rules. Even so, every third employee works some amount of overtime.) The non-state sector is much less restricted. A part of its activities is carried on as full-time jobs that far exceed the length of the workday or workweek usual in the state sector. This is the case with work performed on a family basis in private small-scale industry, in private retail trade and in leased activities, but the lengthening of the worktime (openly or in a concealed manner) is usually accepted by the employees. Many people work the legal hours in the formal sector and continue working in the evening and on week-ends in the informal sector, or in their own household plots, or on their own home-building efforts. Not infrequently, the non-legal practice is that the employee does his "private" work at the place of his main job—in the best case when he has nothing else to do, in the worst case to the detriment of the task to be done at the main job. There is increased participation of family labour: housewives or other members of the family can join the productive activity of the family without restriction, be it agricultural work in the household plot or construction. In the final analysis, the total worktime of the whole population is substantially longer than what is recorded as legal worktime in the formal sector: it is estimated that about 16–18 per cent of the total manhours available are spent in the informal sector.[17]

An appraisal of the situation is difficult. Many people ruthlessly exploit themselves. The extensive lengthening of the individual and family worktime and the increased intensity of work done in the additional worktime can greatly increase the income of the households that make this sacrifice. The additional income can frequently be a multiple of what the employee could earn in the state sector, inclusive of the allowed overtime. A classical subject of microeconomics is the choice between consumption and leisure. There is a widespread, very industrious and self-driven stratum of the Hungarian population that opts for hard work, almost up to the biological limit of capacity or even beyond it in order to get consumption goods. Certainly this is one of the secrets of the frequently mentioned "Hungarian wonder". One of the features of the 1979–82 measures is that it soberly reckons with this choice of a considerable part of the population and tries to remove at least the administrative obstacles for those who are voluntarily lengthening the worktime with the aim of personal gain.

5. DISTRIBUTION BY BRANCHES

Elements of the non-state sector crop up in all branches of economic activity, but not to a uniform extent. Most often cited and best known is its role in agriculture. Apart from that it is important in the services, construction, housing, domestic trading, and to a lesser extent in transport. From that list it is clear that we are dealing with branches whose products are to some degree or other sold for consumption by the general public or for whose products the household represents one of the main buyers. The non-state sphere appears far more sporadically and is far less important in industry in the narrower sense, and within it in manufacture of the means of production. In part this is natural: no one wishes Hungary to adopt the idea China once had of "garden foundries". All sober advocates of the reform recognize that in a modern economy there are many products that can be manufactured economically only in large or even vast plants. So in this case extremely important tasks devolve on the large, state-owned companies. However, there is also scope in industry and in the manufacture of the means of production for the non-state or combined forms that we mentioned earlier in examples of other branches. For instance a small plant might produce quite economically parts or semi-finished products for large, state-owned companies that would produce the end-product. Such small plants might take the form of industrial co-operatives, ancillary plants of co-operative farms, private or state-owned small companies, or small co-operatives. Moreover, a proportion of these tasks could even be done at home as outwork, thus utilizing the labour of those who for family reasons, because of commitments in the household or simply because of dislike of the ties accompanying industrial work are unwilling to go out to work in a factory. These forms of activity do already exist to a comparatively restricted extent. Time will tell whether state-owned industry is capable of opening out for more than it has so far, whether the economic reform can mobilize these forms of co-operation between the state and non-state spheres, or whether the forms known up to now will continue to prevail: large, state-owned companies making as many of their own parts and semi-finished products themselves as they can, or importing them, or buying them from other large companies.

6. GOVERNMENT REGULATION AND DEGREE OF PATERNALISM

In this aspect the non-state sphere is very heterogeneous indeed: its various parts are handled differently by the state. The situation has changed several times in the last 10 or 15 years.

The agricultural co-operatives obtained and continue to get much encouragement from the state. (This can hardly be said about the industrial co-operatives.) Even so, the autonomy of the co-operatives—though much wider than that of state enterprises—is far from complete. Higher state authorities and the central organs of the co-operative network interfere with their operation in many forms. It might be said, though, that the relationship between the state and the co-operative is somewhat less paternalistic than between the state and the state-owned enterprise. The financial position of the co-operative depends more on market success; its survival is not automatically guaranteed (though, if it is in great trouble, there is a chance that the state will save it). Its growth rather considerably depends on its own economic results. Because of all this, *the interest in profits of the co-operative is stronger and its budget constraint is harder than that of the still dominant large state enterprises.*[18]

The other parts of the non-state sphere—the private sector working under state licence, the combined forms of ownership and operation, the informal activities—are characterized by hard budget constraints. Their existence depends on market demand. A unit or an activity survives as long as it produces a profit for its entrepreneur.

But this does not mean that its existence depends exclusively on the market. It depends on the state, on economic policy, as well as on the behaviour of state enterprises and co-operatives. A part of the activities requires official licencing, unless the person pursuing the activity risks illegality. Another part relies on open co-operation with state-owned or co-operative units (e.g. the forms described in rows 1–3 of Table 7, or the household plot linked to the co-operative). Support of the state and co-operative sectors can be given, or official licences may be granted, but they can also be revoked. This is why the non-state sphere is penetrated by an at times weak, at other times stronger feeling of uncertainty. This feeling of uncertainty can be dispelled only by unambiguous experiences of long duration.

5. Interrelation of the economic mechanism with the rate of growth and its proportions

The rate of growth slowed down at the end of the seventies in Hungary, as in many other countries. This paper does not undertake a comprehensive analysis of the causes of the deceleration. I only wish to consider the problem of deceleration to the extent that it is related to the reform of the economic mechanism. We divide the interrelation into two directions of cause and effect. One is the role of the mechanism or rather the reform it has played in the decelerating of growth: the extent to which it contributed to the slowdown, changed the proportions of production and consumption, etc. The contrary direction of influence is how the slowing down of growth and the demand–supply ratio that has now emerged has affected the reform of the economic mechanism.

Let us look at the first theme in connection with it. Of course we cannot embrace this in its entirety either, and we shall only pick out two questions. The first is the examination of *investment*. Let us glance at Table 8. Until 1983 investment in the smaller European socialist countries was growing at roughly similar rates to those in the smaller European capitalist countries. After the price explosion the investment growth rate in the capitalist countries slowed down dramatically, whereas in the socialist countries it continued to grow at the same rate for several years as if nothing had happened. From this point of view the Hungarian economy behaved in basically the same way as those of the other socialist countries. The investment growth rate standstill

TABLE 8

GROWTH OF THE VOLUME OF INVESTMENT
(AVERAGE ANNUAL RATE OF GROWTH IN PERCENTAGE)

	1968–72	1973–77	1978–79
Bulgaria	5.9	9.7	–0.8
Poland	13.3	10.5	–2.8
Hungary	8.0	8.5	2.9
GDR	7.2	6.1	1.8
Austria	7.5	2.5	0.0
Denmark	7.0	2.0	–1.1
Finland	10.9	0.6	–2.4
Greece	7.7	–3.5	5.0
Italy	6.0	4.1	2.2
Spain	9.9	0,4	–1.6

Source: For capitalist countries: data of the UN and the OECD; for socialist countries: national statistical yearbooks.

followed in about 1977. This sequence of events can, I think, be explained as follows:

In the socialist economy decision-makers are motivated by a strong internal expansion drive on every level, from executives to shop foremen. The investment hunger is permanent and almost insatiable.[19] The central agencies are permeated by this drive also, yet they are from time to time held back by macroeconomic considerations. From the ministries and the medium-level authorities, from state enterprises and public institutions, and to a certain extent also from the agricultural co-operatives, there is constant pressure on the centre to give permits, credits and subsidies to the greatest possible number of investment projects. This is closely related to the softness of the budget constraint: the investor does not feel that his decision involves genuine risks. In Western countries investment abated when business prospects became gloomier, beginning with 1973. This acted as a self-generating vicious circle: the brake on the investment impetus made prospects even gloomier. In the socialist countries there was no trace of this after 1973: the investment boom continued. *Despite the reform this fully holds true for Hungary, too.* Through the reform the Hungarian state-owned enterprise obtained greater autonomy in short-term decisions, but since the state continued to act as a "general insurance company", no *inner* inhibition developed against investment hunger in enterprise behaviour. Why should the Hungarian enterprise, and along with it the ministry and the middle-level directing body, not have striven to grab as much investment as it could?

The brake on investment after 1978 was not a spontaneous halt by the enterprises, it was clearly a central action. It was decided and carried out by the highest leadership out of foreign trade and balance of payments considerations and in spite of the unchanged investment hunger of the medium-level and lower executives.

A separate study could be devoted to examining what advantages and disadvantages have stemmed and may stem from the slowdown of growth in investment. Of course, deceleration of investment in itself does not solve any of the economic problems of the Hungarian economy.[20] However, whether or not the sudden deceleration was justified at all, the renewed sudden acceleration of investment intentions has not become justified by any change in economic circumstances. And yet they have gathered momentum again, as if to prove the investment cycle theory of *Bauer* and of others.[21] This does not yet appear in the total amounts of investment, because up to now the centre has withstood the pressure. But the number of newly begun projects grew in 1980–81. Total investment credit requests in 1980 exceeded those of 1979 by 84 per cent, and those in the first three-quarters of 1981 rose by 79 per cent against the same period of the preceding year. The requests for financial state support of investment projects in 1981 are also a multiple of those in the preceding year. At any enterprise where the development resources have grown they strive to spend them as fast as possible on their own investment projects. Once again it is clear that the 1979–82 measures did not really harden the budget constraint of the enterprises. *While economic prospects of the country are uncertain, the enterprises are quite self-confident regarding their investment outlook.*

Even in 1977–78 it was not the market prospects that were found uncertain by the enterprises, but rather the expectation of changes in financial regulators and pricing principles. Now their fears begin to calm down; profit has started to revert to the old level—what should then prompt a *voluntary* suppression of the investment propensity? Enterprises are like war-steeds, which, on hearing the bugle call, would like to gallop, tearing the reins. A new investment rush would certainly have started with full vigour if the centre had not forcibly held it back.

Apart from investment, the other topic I should like to touch on briefly is *consumption* and the standard of living. In the 1973–81 period when the welfare of people suffered gravely in many other countries in East, West and South, the Hungarian population was relatively well off. This was particularly so in the first part of the period, when, in the framework of general growth, consumption also continued to increase. Though the retrenchment following 1977 reduced investment most of all, a part of the reduction—mainly of investment projects in infrastructure—also affected the living circumstances of the population. In the years 1978–80 real wages per earner fell somewhat, but the total volume of consumption did not. Shortages of consumer articles and services did not significantly increase. (We shall return to this later.) What is particularly important from the viewpoint of the public, the food supply is satisfactory, and in some basically important products it is definitely abundant. There are no blockages in the supply to consumers of fuel and energy. This is one of the most important and spectacular achievements of the Hungarian economy.

This achievement may be explained by three factors: (a) the living standard policy as one element in the general economic policy and planning governing the economic proportions, (b) the reform of the regulation mechanism of state enterprises begun in 1968 and developed further in 1977–82, and (c) the continuous growth of the non-state sphere over 15–20 years. These three factors are, of course, closely related. The year 1968 was an important milestone in the development of all three. The extension of the non-state sphere should be regarded as an organic part of the reform process. Yet it is worthwhile to treat these three factors separately.

The traditional view of the source of Hungarian successes in consumer goods supplies stresses factor (b). The typical Western journalist looks at the downtown shops and the market-halls of Budapest, returns home and writes that the shops are full because market socialism is at work in Hungary. In my view the role of this factor is relatively modest, even if it did indeed contribute to the favourable supply situation. The autonomy of the enterprise in short-term decision-making facilitates its adjustment to the demand of the buyer, because it has freed the firm from the bureaucratic restrictions of plan instructions. In a few areas of state-owned industry (food, household chemicals, and in several branches of light industry) a "buyers' market" which stimulates widening of assortment and improvement of quality is about to emerge. (This is, however, far from general.) *But a large part of the Hungarian enterprises of today are not yet forced to compete for the buyer by the economic coercion of market competition.* The enterprise may in many cases be interested in rather giving preference to export, even in cases when export is not particularly profitable and there is a depressing shortage on the domestic market. It manœuvres among the different sales markets according to the conditions of bargaining with the state organs and is not necessarily led by the profit possibilities emerging in the market, thus perhaps pushing the domestic consumer into the background.

The favourable state of supply is due mainly to factors (a) and (c). Factor (a) is important because *for 25 years central economic policy has been "biased" in favour of living standards* and this policy continues even now, in spite of accumulated economic difficulties. To this day no one has ever implemented in Hungary any Draconian austerity programme that sought to eliminate the problems largely at the expense of a drastic fall in living standards. Economic policy, if forced to take measures that affect the consumer's welfare unfavourably, attempts to blunt them and does not wish to proceed far in this direction. When it was decided recently to reduce the domestic use of total net output, this happened primarily at the expense of investment. Central policy-makers frequently protect the domestic consumer market through central measures from the "suction" effect of export, since there do not exist enterprise incentives for adjusting supply automatically to demand.

The other main explanation is factor (c), the operation of the non-state sector. The performance of co-operatives, household plots and complementary farms in supplying the population with food is well known. Other elements of the non-state sphere also contribute much to satisfying the demand of households, and make up for the gaps and shortages left by the state sector. This sphere is *one of the built-in stabilizers of the Hungarian economy of today*. It is relatively insensitive to the decelerations and accelerations of the state sector, to the cyclical fluctuations of investment, and to changes in foreign trade and balance of payments positions. Since to a significant extent it embraces formal and informal market relations within the general population and household consumption of its own produce, it is capable of stabilizing itself and modestly but steadily growing—so long as it is "left in peace", not subjected to administrative restriction unnecessarily, or disturbed by rumours of future intervention.

From these thoughts on investment and consumption a common lesson can be drawn. It is not my intention to belittle the merits of the 1968 reform, but to call attention to the fact that the reform has been only halfway implemented to this very day. A large part of the Hungarian output is contributed by the state sector and this sector is not controlled by a true market mechanism. *There does not exist a built-in mechanism that could assert itself in the behavioural rules of the state enterprise, that could hold it back from the investment drive and that could force it to adjust to demand. The factors that guarantee moderation of growth policy and a favourable internal supply of goods to the population are not sufficiently "institutionalized".* This could only be secured by a really comprehensive reform of the economic mechanism that also deeply permeates the state sector.

Let us turn now to the other direction of influence: how the present growth policy affects the process of reforming the economic mechanism.

The Hungarian economy, similar to the economies of the other socialist countries, has been plagued for years by chronic shortage phenomena. While in quite a few fields this shortage is less severe than in some other socialist countries, still the Hungarian system may be considered a shortage economy to a considerable extent. In Tables 9 and 10 we survey a few indicators of shortage to characterize the situation after 1979. As can be seen, the picture is rather mixed: some indicators improve somewhat, others stay constant, still others deteriorate somewhat. No great "dramatic" change has occurred. On the one hand, in no field has the shortage become greater to any palpable extent. In the given economic situation this might be considered in itself a considerable achievement. On the other hand, while severity of shortage has abated in some fields, on *neither* the investment market, *nor* the markets for labour, means of production or consumer goods has, since 1979, *such progress occurred that the econ-*

TABLE 9
SHORTAGE INDICATORS FOR PRODUCTION

Indicator	Unit of measurement	1976	1977	1978	1979	1980	1981	Evaluation
(1) Share of materials inputs in total manufacturing inventories[a]	Per cent	70	71	72	72	72	–	Unchanged intensity shortage
(2) Ratio of orders refused by construction industry relative to its annual output[b]	Per cent	39.4	41.4	26.5	16.8	16.0	20.8	Improvement in the period 1977–80
(3) Shortage in building materials[c]	Percentage points	1.2	0.6	-3.1	-3.1	-4.5	–	Considerable improvement
(4) Unsatisfied demand for railway transport[d]								Considerable improvement since 1978
Demand but not supplied railroad cars	1,000 units	307.2	306.3	478.3	367.3	159.2	172.2	
Missing transport capacity	Million tonnes	9.1	9.7	15.1	11.6	5.0	5.3	
(5) Partial indicator of labour shortage[e]	Per cent	24	–	35	36	39	–	Shortage diminished in 1978, no improvement since

[a] This ratio is high on the sellers' market (accumulation in input stocks because of shortage); it is low on the buyers' market (swelling of output stocks).

[b] Refers to the construction industry.

[c] Difference between the index numbers of construction activity and the building materials industry supply, relative to the preceding year. The larger the indicator, the greater the shortage. The indicator was worked out by János *Gács*.

[d] Interpretation of these as "shortage indicators" was initiated by Iván *Major*.

[e] Jobs filled by official labour exchanges as percentage of job openings (only part of labour turnover is reported on the exchanges).

Sources: (1) *Fábri* [23], communications by E. Fábri; (2) Reports, Central Statistical Office; (3) *Gács* [33], communication by J. Gács; (4) *Major* [58], communication by I. Major; (5) Communication, State Office for Wages and Labour.

TABLE 10

SHORTAGE INDICATORS FOR CONSUMPTION

Indicator	Unit of measurement	1976	1977	1978	1979	1980	1981	Evaluation
(1) Computed queuing time for dwellings rationed by the state (number of requests for housing, on January 1, divided by allocations during year)	Year	–	7.3	6.8	7.1	7.0	–	No improvement
(2) Computed queuing time for passenger cars (orders on January 1, divided by numbers of cars sold during year)	Year	2.3	2.5	3.6	5.3	3.1	2.4	Improvement since 1979
(3) Number of persons waiting for telephone connections	Persons	233,00	–	267,000	–	–	296,000	Growing shortage
(4) Average length of time required to get serviced (state and co-operative sector only)	Days							
Routine oil and motor check				7.9	–	8.1	–	No major improvement
Repair of collision damage				15.9	–	16.5	–	

	Unit						
Washing of linen (by weight)				11.9	11.0	–	
Washing of linen (by piece)				12.7	10.9	–	
Suit made to order				35.9	35.9	–	
Dress made to order				24.9	24.4	–	
New linoleum				17.9	18.9	–	
Painting of dwelling				21.6	26.8	–	
(5) Average length of hospitalization	Days	14.6	14.6	14.5	14.2	–	About the same
(6) Assessment by public opinion as a cause of difficulties in acquiring supplies (Market researchers put the question: "In your experience day-to-day difficulties in shopping have (a) grown, (b) stayed unchanged, or (c) lessened this year?")	%			(a) 37 (b) 46 (c) 12 unassess-able 5			The population subjectively perceives a stagnation or rise in the intensity of shortage: those sensing a fall were very few

Sources: (1, 4, 5) Reports, Central Statistical Office; (2) Kapitány et al. [47], communication by Merkur Company on the sale of cars; (3) Communication by Post Office General Manager; (6) Communication by K. Farkas and J. Pataki (Mass Communication Centre)

omy would leap from a sellers' market unambiguously into a buyers' market.[22]

There were some who hoped that the mere fact of deceleration of growth could bring about a turning-point. But this has not occurred.

Let us first look at the *demand* side. The official and non-official price rises held demand by the population back somewhat; the financial sources of investment were radically reduced. Still, regarding total demand of the economy, two forces continue to assert themselves: the insatiable *investment hunger,* which tries to break through in many ways, and the "suction" effect of *forced exports.* "We improve the balance of payments," is now the key phrase to obtain short or long-term credits and investment subsidies.

If we are not reasoning merely in macro aggregates, but observe some individual markets, we find that *demand has decreased in several fields, but so has supply.* There are several factors working in this direction. Import possibilities have declined, for example, in regard to raw materials and primary energy from the CMEA countries. This shortage on the input side can place a limit on production. The importation of some consumer articles has been braked. Financial and moral incentives may have promoted a restriction in supply. The so-called "competitive price system", as I have already pointed out, might have made enterprises interested in restricting their volume of output.

Whereupon one can ask which of the two directions of influence and casual relationships was the basic and decisive one. I consider the primary problem is that the 1979–82 period still has not secured the consistent enforcement of the reform principles in the state sector. This is why it has not happened that hard constraints have limited demand, or strong stimulation is felt for increasing supply. The scissors of demand and supply could not open up. Of course, this leads to a second consequence: the survival of the sellers' market puts a brake on the development of true competition. *The slowdown does not provide for a leap of the economy from a sellers' market to a buyers' market; artificial stimulation of the market does not replace genuine market competition.*

6. Forces and counterforces

This would be the place to speak about the prospects of the reform; as a matter of fact, this was promised by the title of the paper. But a clear forecast cannot be given because the outcome of the fight between the forces for and against the reform is uncertain. Let us take the major factors in turn.

1. The future development of *external conditions,* from outside the Hungarian frontiers, will have a great impact. Will there be reforms in the other socialist countries, or will the Hungarian experiment remain isolated? What will be the role of the linkage with the CMEA countries in the supply of Hungary with raw materials and energy; how will trading and other economic relations with these countries develop? How will the situation of the world economy develop and, in this context, what will be the possibilities for Hungarian exports and the conditions of financing our imports? What will be the international political atmosphere and, depending on it, what will be the defence burdens of Hungary? We cannot give a prediction of the development of external circumstances and, as a matter of fact, without those, it is impossible to forecast the internal processes unambiguously.

2. Passing now to the internal forces, how does the *"apparatus"* behave toward the reform process—meaning the officials in responsible jobs of the political and administrative agencies and the managers of the economy? My impression is that their attitude toward the reform process is not uniform and that many officials are ambivalent about it. One of the hopes for the reform is rooted in the fact that it has many convinced adherents in the general staff of the economy who try to improve the mechanism and fight resistance to it with great expertise, inventiveness and perseverance. About the resistance it must be said that nowadays the wind blows in the direction of the reform; open opposition against it is rare and weak. Yet it is difficult to make progress, since every step of true decentralization or deregulation deprives various groups of the influence hitherto exercised. How could they be expected to adopt the principle of *"heraus mit uns"* (out with us)? If the winds would blow again against the reform, these forces would become much more active.

3. Ambivalence is particularly strong among the *executives of large state enterprises*. The majority of them have an aversion to central tutelage, and would like to achieve true autonomy, inclusive of wider rights to export and import independently, to fix prices and wages, and so on. They are irritated by the complicated and volatile changes of the "regulatory system". At the same time, they are grateful if the state yields to pressure and helps them in case of financial failure and they would not like to lose the privilege of this safety.[23]

Large enterprises objected sharply to the 1982 measures on small enterprises because the small firm, in whatever form it operates, might be an uncomfortable competitor. In places it may also provide competition for sales, although a considerable defence against this is provided by the chronic shortages. It would be even more dangerous if the less restricted small firm would have an advantage in procuring inputs, especially of labour, as against the large enterprise, which is shackled by many rules. While this might strengthen the demand on the part of the large enterprises that they, too, should be given greater autonomy and fewer rules, it might also turn them against the small firm. Similarly, in quite a few enterprises and state organs aversion and even opposition to the formation of the "economic working teams" is found.

One hopes that finally everywhere the kind of peaceful coexistence and even co-operation will evolve that developed in agriculture between large and small establishments and between state and non-state spheres. For the time being, however, the relationships are still unclear.

4. The reluctance to accept the reforms caused by *ideological conservatism and orthodoxy,* though closely related to the resistance caused by fear for losing influence and privileges, is a separate factor. It might show itself also on the part of people who are not affected as individuals by the reform. Foreign analyses frequently underline approvingly—and with justification—that the Hungarian reformers are pragmatic: instead of ideologizing, they implement changes. But one should not believe that everybody is "pragmatic" in Hungary. Many have the feeling that the reform has already relinquished ideals sanctioned by the traditions of the socialist movement; they would become even more indignant if the market, profit, competition, non-state ownership, and, among the various forms of the latter, private

ownership would obtain a wider scope.[24] Hungary proceeds along an untrodden path. Who can tell where is the critical point at which ideological aversion blocks the process of transformation?

Besides, it cannot be denied that the kind of mixed economy that now characterizes Hungary, and will characterize it even more if the reform is to proceed further, resembles a hot furnace that produces iron and slag simultaneously. Achievements are unavoidably accompanied by negative consequences such as the chase after money, ruthless self-exploitation, clever manœuvring and corruption. These harmful phenomena, particularly if they are not sufficiently fought against, strengthen the arguments of those who are on an ideological basis against the reform of the socialist economy.

5. *Income distribution* is an important factor in the formation of public opinion. Public opinion polls show that a considerable part of the Hungarian society would like an income distribution more egalitarian than the present one.[25] It seems that this is not a highly explosive gripe, but rather a disapproval of the existing situation. But who knows whether this remains so in the future? Public opinion may change if inequalities are growing; as a matter of fact, a consistent progress of the reform would presumably entail that. Even more important: society might react to inequality much more sharply if the general standard of living is stagnating or declining. *Hirschman* [43] excellently characterized the problem with his tunnel analogy. If there are two parallel lanes in the tunnel and we perceive that our lane has stopped but the other is proceeding, we are initially inclined to consider this as a reassuring sign. It seems there is not a complete stoppage at the end of the tunnel: our lane, too, would also start soon. But if traffic is persistently smooth on the lane beside us and, nevertheless, our own has got stuck for some longer time, we sooner or later lose our patience and try to cross into the other lane. If the income of some people is rising more rapidly than that of others, but everybody's income is rising anyway, this is usually tolerated by society. But if the income of people with low resources does not rise or even declines, while that of others conspicuously rises, the limit of tolerance of society may suddenly sink lower. Therefore, the fate of the reform depends much on whether a general rise of living standards would resume.

Many other factors will influence the future of the reform. But even if we considered all these, I doubt that we could arrive at a more unambiguous prediction. What is unambiguous is the hope of this author that the cause of the reform will not get stuck but will further proceed and our efforts too contribute to that process.

NOTES

[1] Unfortunately not all the comprehensive assessments of the latest phase in the reform process or basic analysis of the important relations are available. Reports worth paying attention to have been prepared by several state organizations—the National Planning Office, the Ministry and the Central Statistical Office, for instance. At state or party commission several committees exist to examine Hungary's economic situation from one angle or another, and these prepare written reports containing their findings and proposals. I have read several thousand pages of analyses and reports and spoken with many leading figures in the economy. The information assembled often from divergent points of view does not present itself unambiguously. I have heard or read many observations that contradict one another. Nonetheless I have attempted to draw inferences and formulate general conclusions. I cannot claim that the conclucions expressed in the study are indisputably supported by the facts, but perhaps they may, even in their present, semi-verified forms, still contribute to clarifying the current problems of the reform.

In collecting the data for the study I was assisted by several colleagues at the Institute, principally by Péter Pete; I should like here to thank them for their co-operation.

[2] I shall not go into the practical details of the measures taken in 1979–82 or into those of the price regulations of 1980.

[3] The first lessons of the computations were reviewed in the article by *Falubíró–Gálik* [24] and the results of a later investigation by a memorandum of *Mohos* [63]. These are valuable works giving food for thought, and analyse the problem on the basis of rich factual material. In my paper I use only a few summary figures.

[4] Here and in what follows the term "exports" means "exports sold for *convertible currency* on capitalist markets".

[5] New regulations allow for exceptions which will be dealt with below.

[6] This asserts itself particularly strongly in the so-called "follower" enterprises of the competitive price system, and much more with the units that have not been drawn into the competitive pricing system.

[7] *Non-competitive, "follower"*. The price measures introduced in 1978–81 distinguish the production sphere in which the Hungarian product competes

with imported products, or at least may compete with them, in which the Hungarian product is exported or at least may be exported, from the sphere in which neither import nor export competition can appear. The latter non-tradable sphere is known in the Hungarian jargon as non-competitive, and to it belongs, for instance, construction and a large proportion of services.

Within the competitive sphere prices are principally set by firms that have, according to set principles of calculation, a sizeable role in foreign trade, these being the "leader" companies. To the prices of these are adjusted the prices of the other, "follower", companies. (*)

[8] This suggests a possible explanation for the reversion of profitabilities to pre-1979 levels, reported in Table 1 : there are enterprises that by the nature of their production have difficulty in evading some price fixing or calculation rule, while others can easily do that.

[9] In this research project, which is directed by the author, Andrea Deák, Ágnes Matits, Anna Ferge and Miklós Locsmándi participate. How taxes and subsidies were changed among individual state enterprises is also investigated on the basis of the 1976–80 data on all state-owned enterprises.

[10] Profit-sharing is in proportion to wages and expressed in terms of how many days' wages it represents.

[11] On the subject of the "hardness" and "softness" of budget constraint, see the first and second studies in this volume.

[12] A wealth of statistical material on small-scale farming can be found in the study of *Cseresné* [16]. Zsuzsa Cseres assisted me in compiling the table. The household plot of a member of a co-operative farm is the land which by virtue of his terms of membership is his own personal property to cultivate himself, and may not exceed 0.6 ha. in size. An auxiliary farm is possessed and farmed privately by a village resident *who does not belong to the co-operative farm,* and may not exceed 0.6 ha. in size.

[13] The Hungarian literature on the problems of the non-state sphere is rich indeed. Agricultural co-operatives, household and auxiliary plots are discussed by *Donáth* [22] and *Cseresné* [16]. The "second economy" is analysed in *Gábor* [31], *Gábor–Galasi* [32] and *Kolosi* [50]. In drafting this paper I used their ideas—and also different reports on the second economy. But in the paper I have not used the term itself. Many data of Section 4 of this paper have been taken from the works of Kolosi and Gábor and Galasi. Finally, a third group of works reviews and evaluates the 1982 rules relating to the small enterprises. The most complete survey is offered by *Szép* [78].

[14] In the subtitle of the first paragraph I have juxtaposed self-sufficiency and "work done for others" and not production for the market, because the latter can be carried on not only in "business" units producing for the market, but also in non-profit institutions.

[15] *Child-care allowance* was introduced in Hungary in 1967. By this move the

government sought to offer working mothers with small children the chance to take unpaid leave from work till the child's third birthday, during which time she would receive a fixed sum of allowance amounting to 20–25% of the average wage. The original regulation disallowed the acceptance of work during the time the allowance was being received. This stipulation was modified in 1982, and the mother may now take on a maximum of four hours' work a day so long as the child has reached the age of 18 months, without forfeiting the child-care allowance. (*)

[16] Tibor Liska has expounded his entrepreneurial concept in several studies. A more detailed discussion of the problem is to be found in an article of *Bársony* [7].

[17] See *Markó* [59].

[18] As a matter of fact, it is not exact to compare the *whole* co-operative sector to the *whole* of the sector of large state enterprises. A medium or a small enterprise in an industrial branch which is less in the foreground may be perhaps similarly left to itself, as is an average industrial co-operative. The most favoured large agricultural co-operative, however, is treated in the same paternalistic manner as the huge state-owned enterprise.

[19] See *Kornai* [51], Chapter 9.

[20] This is discussed in detail in *Nyers–Tardos* [68]. I agree with their appraisal.

[21] See first of all a book of *Bauer* [9]. See also articles by *Soós* [74], *Bauer* [8] and *Lackó* [54]. In the analysis of the present investment situation I was helped by Mária Lackó.

[22] In the wake of the brake on investment, it is mostly the construction industry that has come nearer to the state of a "buyers' market". (See Table 9.) Many construction enterprises now make efforts to please the buyer: they are more willing to undertake renewals, which they earlier warded off, to initiate export activity and so forth. But, for the behaviour of the construction industry to change more deeply, for it to really subordinate itself to the demands of the buyer so that, in consequence, the buildings would be ready more quickly and be of better quality, the "buyers' market" has to persist for a somewhat longer time.

[23] The recentralization efforts of the large enterprises are discussed in *Szalai* [76].

[24] For example, several strata of the population support private plots. But there are also strong reservations revealed in the interviews by *Kispista* [49]: "I sincerely say, I look with anxiety at the spreading of the small-scale production so much propagandized..."—"...now that the reins have been loosened, small-scale production is blooming. But this is very dangerous in the long run."—"...This only happens because we are dependent on it. It is a forced solution. We have to dispose of it, the sooner the better."

[25] In its public opinion polls the Mass Communications Centre repeatedly asked the question whether differentiation of incomes should be reduced or increased in Hungary. For the reductions were 56% in 1973, 69% in 1974 and 65% in 1976 (only in Budapest), 63% in 1979 and 60% in 1980. For an increase of differentiation, in the same order of years: 28, 14, 14, 18 and 21%. Considering the differences between the samples taken and different times, we may say that the distribution is rather stable, or at least does not show any definite tendency. (See *Angelusz–Pataki* [1], *Nagy–Angelusz–Tardos* [65], *Farkas–Pataki* [27] and *Nagy–Virágh* [66].)

Efficiency and the Principles of Socialist Ethics*

Two systems of values

The 1968 economic reform brought tangible results.[1] During the ten years following the reform, production grew strongly and fairly steadily. There is full employment. Since reserve labour has been almost entirely absorbed, the growth of production mainly reflects rising labour productivity.

Although it would be worth analysing the results achieved since the reform in more detail, it is not these that I wish to discuss, but rather some of the difficulties and problems of the Hungarian economy. Hungarian economists are in a privileged position to observe an experiment, unique in history. I feel that it is our duty to provide information on the experience of this experiment, and not only on the spectacular successes but on the less conspicuous difficulties as well.

One of the aims of the reform was to render the functioning of Hungarian economy more efficient. In the following I shall enumerate *some of the necessary conditions for economic efficiency*.[2] I do not strive for completeness: certainly quite a few important conditions will be left out of the list. I do not undertake, either, to reduce the conditions of efficiency to a small number of *final* conditions, that is, to discuss the question in an axiomatic form. Instead, I rest content with discussing five conditions which have often been the subject of dispute in relation to the Hungarian reform.

* First journal publication in English: "The Dilemmas of a Socialist Economy: the Hungarian Experience", Cambridge Journal of Economics, Vol. 4 (1980), pp. 147–157. (Copyright by Academic Press Inc. [London] Ltd.) The paper was originally delivered as the Twelfth Geary Lecture, 1979, at The Economic and Social Research Institute, Dublin.

(1) A material and moral *incentive* system is needed which stimulates better performance from all individuals participating in production—leaders and workers alike.

(2) Careful *calculation* must be made which takes into account benefits and costs. Scarce resources must be used economically. Non-efficient production activities must be terminated.

(3) There must be fast and flexible *adjustment* to the current situation and external conditions.

(4) Decision-makers must display *entrepreneurship* through their initiative, disposition for innovation and risk-taking.

(5) Every decision-maker must assume *personal responsibility* for the matters in his or her charge and for decisions.

There is not any particular "socialist" content in the above-listed five conditions. Yet they cannot be considered as "capitalist" ones, either. They are *principles of general validity* for efficient management and organization. The official economic conception of Eastern European countries has always acknowledged—not only since the reform, but earlier, too—these requirements as the necessary conditions for economic development and for raising labour productivity.

Another group of values may be called briefly: *the ethical principles of a socialist economy*. Again I do not strive for completeness; quite a number of known principles have been left out of the list. Similarly, as in talking about efficiency, I do not try to give an axiomatic formulation or to establish a few *final* postulates. I shall confine myself to putting forward four principles. They may even partly overlap. In any case, their importance is justified by the fact that they have great practical influence in economic life. All four principles arose at the dawn of the labour movement within the frames of the capitalist system, but later they were reappraised under socialist economic conditions, when, a new or, in some cases, modified interpretation was placed upon them. This study deals exclusively with the interpretation placed upon them *at present* in Hungary.

(a) The well-known principle of *socialist wage-setting:* "to everybody according to his work".[3] This includes the other well-known distribution principle: "equal pay for equal work". Although the first expression of this latter principle was based on the wage demands of women, minorities and other groups in a disadvantageous position, the interpretation placed on it in the socialist economy has widened.

Clearly a consistent application of distribution according to work must be accompanied by the same payment for work of the same quantity and quality.

(b) Principle of *solidarity*. Socialism eliminates the cruelty of capitalist competition, which casts out the weak. The weak must not be punished for their weakness. On the contrary, they must be helped to rise.

(c) Principle of *security*. Each member of society should feel secure. This principle is closely connected with the preceding principle (b). Some of its important implications are as follows.

(i) The individual or small community gains a feeling of security by knowing that, when in trouble, he or they can count on the help of the large community.

(ii) Society provides full employment, not only momentarily, but once and for all. Fear of unemployment ceases.

(iii) The same thing can be said not only of full employment but, more generally, of every achievement. The feeling of security is further strengthened by the fact that the level once attained is also guaranteed for the future by society.

(d) *Priority of general interest* over partial interest, whether the latter is that of an individual, or of a small community. This principle implies priority of the long-term interest of several consecutive generations over the exclusive short-time interest of today's generation.

Among economists of socialist conviction the view has taken root that there is no contradiction between the two value systems—efficiency and socialist ethical values. Perhaps this idea was expressed most forcefully in the classical study on the theory of socialism written by the great Polish economist, Oscar *Lange*.[4] Lange presents a decentralized market economy along Walrasian lines, which functions efficiently and, at the same time, fits without difficulty into a social system built on socialist principles.

This traditional interpretation is not justified in the light of experience. It seems that *conflicts are inevitable between the conditions (1)–(5) of efficiency, on the one hand, and the ethical principles (a)–(d) of a socialist economy on the other*. Numerous decision-making dilemmas of the socialist economy are caused precisely by the clash of these two different value systems.[5]

Let me add a personal remark here. Although I try to be as objective as possible in analysing the problems of the Hungarian economy, it is almost inevitable that my subjective viewpoint should emerge. On the one hand, I am an economist and, in my other works, I deal with mathematical economics. It is no wonder if my thinking has been "spoiled" by such principles as "rationality" and "efficiency", and by theories of the beneficial effects of decentralized markets. On the other hand, my thinking has been deeply influenced by socialist social and ethical ideals. Therefore, I feel as my own the dilemmas that face every economist concerned with the actual conditions of the Hungarian economy.

We shall examine three classes of problem: (i) incentive linked to profit, (ii) the survival of the firm, and (iii) the growth of the firm. In these areas, the conflicts appear to be particularly sharp between the two value systems: efficiency conditions and socialist ethical principles.

I should like to say in advance that this study does not offer a *causal* analysis. It would be a mistake to believe that the desire to realize ethical principles was the main reason for the infringement of efficiency conditions. Of course the behaviour of the institutions or individuals making decisions is to some extent influenced by moral considerations, but the roots of society's essential regulation of economic behaviour are deeper than that. The theme of this article is much narrower: it does not provide an explanatory theory, only an attempt to analyse *the possibility of harmonizing the two systems of values*.

Incentive linked to profit

One of the most characteristic efforts of the Hungarian reform was to strengthen material incentive linked to the profit of the firm. That would serve to meet all five efficiency conditions, but particularly the first two, namely the development of an incentive system, and careful calculation involving a strict comparison of benefits and costs.

Experience shows, however, that profit incentive clashes with ethical principle (a) which prescribes that everybody should have his share in material goods "according to his work", and that there should be "equal pay" for "equal work".

In Hungarian firms, workers' profit-sharing has been introduced. This is in itself sufficient to infringe principle (a). The total earning of two workers — of identical performance and receiving identical wages — may be different if one receives more through profit-sharing and the other less. What is more, Hungarian firms have more independence in wage setting. The more profitable firm may pay more not only through profit-sharing, but also by higher wages, than the less profitable one. For these reasons the earnings of workers of identical performance may differ significantly.

Let us take an example. Firm G is more profitable than firm H. This may reflect the better work of managers and workers in firm G: discipline is stronger, they pay more attention to the quality of products and adjust more flexibly to external circumstances and, *therefore*, get more profit. It is also possible, however, that the larger profit of the firm is not through their own efforts. Several factors — independent of them — may play a role. For example, firm G has inherited better machinery from the pre-reform period than the less lucky firm H. Or, while the selling prices of their products are centrally set for both, it so happens that those set for firm G contain a high profit margin, while those for firm H contain a low one. Or, both firms are exporting, and world market prices have changed favourably for firm G and unfavourably for firm H.

The managers and workers of firm H will feel that the established proportions of earnings are "unjust". It is not because of their poor work that they have little or no profit — why then should they be punished? Therefore, they try to put pressure upon higher authorities to equalize earnings. The higher authorities themselves often feel that it is wrong to tolerate any serious inequality, since that would contradict the egalitarian traditions of the socialist movement and the acknowledged principle of "equal pay for equal work".

For the levelling trend, numerous means are available. First of all, there are rules of general validity which prescribe in what way the gross profit of the firm should be divided among taxes and other payments to central and local authorities, investment and welfare funds remaining with the firm, and amounts payable by way of profit-sharing and wage increase. Complicated and rather sophisticated formulae are prescribed, guided by various considerations — including income equality. This makes the incentive system less transparent, which in itself diminishes the incentive effect. But that is not all. Intermittent *ad hoc* intervention into the financial situation of the firms is widespread, in order to tax away incomes that are "too high", or to compensate for losses suffered because of "objective difficulties". In the long run, almost two-thirds of the gross profit of firms has been taxed away and redistributed in past years.

The frequent unforeseeable and incalculable redistribution flowing through a hundred channels makes profit incentive illusory from several aspects. In micro-economics, it is assumed that the expenses of the profit-maximizing firm are delimited by the so-called budget constraint. Yet, in the circumstances described above *the budget constraint of the firm "softens"; it does not really bind decisions of the firm.*[6] *The firm can go beyond the budget constraint without any grave consequences. If it suffers financial losses because of uncovered expenses, the state will sooner or later cover these.*

If a firm gets into difficulties—through, for example, reasons beyond its control, such as external difficulties—it may react in two different ways. One is to face the difficulties. This may not be successful, and the firm may fail. And, even if successful, it demands sacrifice. As long as the difficulties of the firm have not been overcome and losses are incurred, earnings are less than in more successful firms. The purpose of the first approach is to adjust *production* as flexibly as possible to the real conditions. The other approach is to ask for help from the higher authorities. The firm sends delegates who complain and "cry". Lobbying begins: the firm tries to get support for its case in the political and social organizations and in the upper-level state offices. Personal connections are used. The purpose of the second approach is to get *financial help:* as much government subsidy, tax allowances and "soft" credit as possible, and as soon as possible.

As a result of the second approach, the firm which had been given much autonomy by the reform subjects itself, almost voluntarily, to patronage. By asking for help it confirms its dependence on the financial organizations, the banks, the price office—in short, on all central institutions that can influence its financial situation.

I should mention here the effect of the income levelling tendency on the entrepreneurial spirit, which figured as the fourth condition of efficiency. Innovation—whether it be a new product, a new technology, a new organization or the penetration of a new market—involves risk. Those who do not succeed will lose. Therefore, it is worth trying only if success brings a *large* gain. In post-reform Hungary the economic leader cannot lose a lot, but in the same way he cannot gain a lot either. There is no scope for any great advance. The firm with uncommon and provocatively high profit will be sooner or later "tapped". The levelling of incomes involves more or less also the levelling of performance.

These are the first examples of conflicts between efficiency conditions and the ethical principles of a socialist economy. *The harder the budget constraint of the firm, the more the earnings of managers and workers of the firm depend on actual profitability, the more the firm can break away from the wage-setting principles related solely to individual work, so that "unjust" differences in earnings may appear. On the other hand, the more the principle of "equal pay for equal work" is asserted, the more the stimulating effect of profit incentive will be weakened.*

Survival of the firm

The next subject of our analysis, namely, the survival of the firm, is closely related to the preceding one. We set down as the second principle of efficiency that, if the comparison of benefits and costs shows an activity to be inefficient, it must cease in the interests of efficiency of the economy as a whole. This must be done even if it causes a serious loss of prestige for the firm's managers, and possible temporary unemployment for its workers.

This condition can come into conflict with ethical principles (b) and (c). According to the principle of solidarity, a weaker community must not be allowed to fail. Rather, it should be supported so that it can continue its activity and rise. And, according to the principle of security, no single member of society need fear failure. Everyone should feel secure that the personal achievements once attained—such as the availability of uninterrupted work—should be guaranteed also for the future. In particular—and this is where our subject is related to that of the previous section—they should feel secure where the troubles are not due to their own fault, but perhaps to external conditions beyond their control.

During the first ten years of the reform in the Hungarian economy practically no bankruptcy occurred: no firm operating with losses was fully liquidated. Workers are guaranteed not only employment, but even employment in their present job. Following the price explosion on the world market not a single Hungarian firm went bankrupt. Using the popular expression in Hungary: the state budget "took over" the losses. The "natural selection" entailed by economic competition did not take place: the strong and the weak, the active and the passive, the innovative and the incompetent all survived the storm.

The state can rescue the firm on the brink of ruin by various methods. It grants special subsidies; if the product in question has a fixed price, it allows a price increase out of turn; it grants tax exemption or duty concessions to the firm, the bank permits credit at favourable terms or allows postponement of repayment, etc.

There is no way to judge clearly the resulting situation. Solidarity and security are in themselves great values. The life of the firm, and the life of the people working for the firm, become more secure, since fear of any vital danger is removed. The same phenomenon, however, inevitably induces an easy-going, lazy attitude. If the firm's survival is automatically guaranteed, the personal responsibility of leaders is obscured, thereby violating the fourth condition of efficiency.

Since it is a related problem, I shall mention at this point also the security of individual employment. The Hungarian economic system freed the workers from the nightmare of unemployment, which not only causes grave financial losses to the society and to the individual, but also debases human dignity, forcing workers to humble themselves before the employers. The elimination of unemployment is an achievement of great historical importance. But then we must face the fact that guaranteed full employment, with its accompaniment of chronic labour shortage, also has drawbacks. People are not all alike: some are more dutiful than others, there are the industrious and the lazy, those who do their work with care and those who neglect it. The fact that the labour market is a "sellers' market" creates a favourable position not only for the former but also for the latter. The manager of a workshop or plant will think twice before he sacks a careless worker, since it is not at all sure that another will be found to replace him. And, even if fired, the worker does not really feel punished, because it is usually easy for him to find a new job.

These closely interdependent phenomena—guaranteed survival of the firm and guaranteed individual jobs—lead to very difficult and deep-rooted problems. Can a society achieve high efficiency exclusively by means of *positive* material and moral incentives, that is by rewarding good work? Are *negative* economic incentives—the fear of failure, and of individual material and moral loss—dispensable? For my own part I am not certain of the answer.

This much seems certain: that here we are faced again with grave dilemmas, the conflicts of different value systems. *There is contradiction between the efficiency conditions on the one side, and the ethical principles of solidarity and security on the other.*

Growth of the firm

Our next subject is the growth of the firm and, in this context, the allocation of investment. Here the conflict of the various efficiency conditions and the ethical principles is manifest in a possibly even more complicated form than in the two fields previously analysed.

Let us start from a hypothetical system, in which the investment decision has been perfectly decentralized. This system would certainly have some advantages from the viewpoint of efficiency. Conditions (3), (4) and (5) would be more vigorously asserted: the entrepreneurial spirit would strengthen, together with initiative and the propensity to innovate. Adjustment would become more flexible. Personal responsibility for investment decisions would be less ambiguous.

Yet, even ignoring for the time being the ethical aspect, perfect decentralization would come into conflict with one or another of the efficiency conditions. First of all, it would clash with the second condition concerned with the calculation of benefits and costs, if we interpret these categories broadly. We would be faced with a well-known problem of welfare economics. A perfectly decentralized market—without any government or other social intervention—does not count the external effects of local decisions that are not reflected in market prices: and this holds whether we are considering either external benefits or external costs. This consideration leads on to ethical principle (d)—priority of social interest. If every firm decides on investment according to its own profit interest, then some projects with major external benefits may be suppressed, while others with major external costs may proceed.

Aware of this dilemma, the Hungarian reform of 1968 decided that responsibility for investment decisions should be divided between the higher and the lower levels of management. A considerable degree of decentralization was envisaged as compared with the pre-reform period, but a large amount of authority was still left in the hands of central institutions. Thus, for example, in 1976 almost half of total investment in the economy was allocated by central decisions. The balance, accounting for a little over half the total, is classified as "investment of firms", because it is initiated by the firm and, formally, the investment decision is made by the firm. But only half of the so-called "investment of firms" is financed exclusively from the firm's own savings. Thus only about a quarter of total investment can be considered as fully decentralized. For the other quarter, the firm has to seek government subsidy or long-term credit, which means that the central planning and financial organization, the bank and the firm take part jointly in these investment decisions.[7]

The established arrangement, involving a combination of centralization and decentralization, has numerous advantages. Where fully decentralized investments would result in unfavourable proportions from the overall social viewpoint, the central authorities can counterbalance these by centrally decided investments. In this way, the allocation of total investment may be adjusted satisfactorily to the central plans, without the need for central allocation of all investment resources down to the last penny.

It may be seen, therefore, that, in the case of a conflict, the centre has the means to assert priority of social interest over local interest or over the interest of the firm. The centre can serve the long-term interests of society—not always expressible in terms of money—as opposed to the short-term profit interest of the firm.

This sharing of decision-making authority allows the use of many different sources of information in preparing for any particular decision. Firms provide the specific partial information and the higher authorities participating in the decision-making process provide the comprehensive view of economy-wide interrelations and of long-term plans.

Yet the advantages are accompanied also by certain disadvantages. Since the majority of investments need central financial subsidy or credit, decision-making is preceded by a lengthy bureaucratic process. This reduces the flexibility of adjustment, involving infringement of the third efficiency condition.

The firms and lower-level authorities try to influence higher authorities. They argue their case, but may also use personal connections, if they feel that this will promote the investment project initiated or supported by them. Economists and planners working in the central authorities are not impersonal representatives of overall social rationality—they are not the philosophers of Plato's ideal state endowed with wisdom soaring above society. They are real people living in the midst of society, linked by a thousand threads to their colleagues active in economic life. It is impossible to know what role is played in their decisions by the strictly rational propositions of economic calculations, as compared with personal motives, which perhaps are subsequently rationalized. Those in the higher authorities who make decisions about investments should always pay special attention to the external effects of projects not reflected in the calculation of the relevant firm. This consideration, however, is often dimmed by considerations advanced by the internal interests of the firm involved.

We must understand the sociology as well as the social psychology of the investment decision process in order to answer also the question: what happens if an investment fails? It is simply impossible to find out who is responsible for the wrong decision. Since decision-making was preceded by a multi-stage iterative process—both in the assembly of information and in the preparation of decision-making—every participating organization and person is responsible. They are responsible—and yet they are not. They can say that they did not really want the investment in this particular form, but that they were forced to compromise with the other participants. Ultimately, therefore, personal responsibility for investment decision-making is lost, in violation of the fifth efficiency condition.

We have now arrived at one explanation of the phenomenon treated in an earlier part of this paper, namely, that the state helps out of difficulties the firm suffering losses. It is not simply an impersonal "state" that helps but rather the use of state resources for this purpose by all the officials participating in the original action through collective decision-making. Let us suppose that a wrong investment decision was in fact the cause of the losses. Construction work has been protracted, machines and buildings cost more than expected, the goods produced by the new capacity and intended for export cannot be sold at the price envisaged, etc. Who will pay for this? Every participant in the decision has an interest in ensuring that the question of responsibility will not be pressed. The fact alone largely explains why the troubled firm has to be helped out.

The situation regarding the allocation of investment is also closely connected with the two types of problems discussed earlier in the paper. As I have mentioned, only a small part of investment is implemented through self-financing or from such credit as the bank would allow by considering only expected profits. Government subsidy or long-term credit may be granted also to firms in a bad financial situation. Therefore, the firm becomes aware that neither its survival, nor even its growth, depends strictly on profitability. This is one of the most important explanations of the phenomenon we denoted as "the softening of the budget constraint". In implementing the investment decision, the firm can go beyond the financial resources available currently or in the near future, without too much risk. The loss will sooner or later be covered by the state. This may lead then to thoughtless investment initiatives, and to wasteful implementation, which again harm efficiency.

Let us sum up what has been said. *On the one hand, there is the ethical principle (d), stating that social interest must be given priority over partial interest. Adherence to this principle is one of the main reasons why the decision-making responsibilities of the firm or of the local institution are limited in the allocation of investment. In order to represent the social interest, the central authorities retain a wide sphere of authority. But the practical application of the principle often conflicts with the other side, i.e. with the conditions of efficiency. In addition, ethical principle (d) is not enforced consistently; partial interest will prevail again and again, even when it is definitely contrary to the common interest of society.*

A few concluding remarks

We have considered three interrelated issues: the questions of profit incentive, and those of survival and growth of the firm. We have seen how the different efficiency conditions and ethical principles may come into conflict. What has been said has been intended to indicate the *dilemmas* themselves, which face Hungarian economic life, rather than how these dilemmas are to be solved. Since the Hungarian experience cannot be "advertised" as having found the way to eliminate every intricate contradiction, we can speak less of the resolution of the dilemmas. Indeed, it may even be one of the best qualities of Hungarian practice in recent years that it has not sought at all to create the illusion of having found a final solution, but assumes the task of experimenting and exploring ways and means.

There are no "pure" and perfectly "consistent" societies. Every real system is built upon the practical compromises of mutually contradictory principles and requirements. This is characteristic also of the Hungarian post-reform situation. In the better case—which is, luckily, rather frequent—the compromise is a "convex combination" of contradictory principles and requirements. The beneficial effect of all the principles involved in the given process is asserted, at least partially. In the worst case, however—which is not infrequent, either—there is no "convexity". Two principles clash: the exclusive application of either would involve disadvantages, but also significant advantages; yet their combination manifests the disadvantages of both conspicuously, and suppresses their advantages. Such a blend of principles and requirements often develops, in which efficiency and ethics are both lost at the same time. In some cases, the combination of a decentralized market—geared towards efficiency—and central intervention—to take account of socialist ethics—can operate in such a way as to mutually extinguish their separate beneficial effects.

Reformers of economic institutions and mechanisms are prone to "perfectionism". Seeing the first weak points, they wish to reform the reform continuously. For example, during the eleven years that have passed since the 1968 reform, over one hundred orders and legal rules were issued to regulate the profit and profit-sharing of the firm. However well-considered and ingenious some of them may be, the incessant search for perfection is precisely what undermines their effect. Participants cannot train themselves well in the game if the rules are constantly changing. Therefore, we have come to face a new dilemma: the institutional framework—as yet only half-proved—cannot settle down because of uncertainty generated by the constant search for perfection and the disadvantages of the resulting instability.

The tradition of economics has accustomed us to the concept that everything can and must be "optimized". It is therefore understandable that the idea arose that an "optimum economic system" must be designed, combining the best possible "rules of game" and the best operating control mechanisms. Those setting this aim envisage something like a visit to a supermarket. On the shelves are to be found the various components of the mechanism, incorporating the advantageous qualities of all systems. On one shelf, there is full employment as it has been realized in Eastern Europe. On another, there is the high degree of workshop organization and discipline, like in a West German or Swiss factory. On a third shelf is economic growth free of recession, on a fourth, price stability, on a fifth, rapid adjustment of production to demands on the foreign market. The system designer has nothing to do but push along his trolley and collect these "optimum components", and then compose from them at home the "optimum system".

But that is a naïve, wishful day-dream. History does not provide such supermarkets in which we can make our choice as we like. Every real economic system constitutes an organic whole. They may contain good and bad features, and more or less in fixed proportions. The choice of system lies only among various "package deals". It is not possible to pick out from the different "packages" the components we like and to exclude what we dislike.[8]

It seems to me that *it is impossible to create a closed and consistent socio-economic normative theory which would assert, without contradiction, a politico-ethical value system and would at the same time provide for the efficiency of the economy.*[9] *It is impossible if that theory seeks to be realistic and wishes to take into account the true behavioural characteristics of people, communities, organizations and social groups.*

It is more important and more pressing to observe existing societies, and to find an explanation for their behavioural regularities. Our science has to find the answer to the question: what compromises between the different normative principles are brought about by the social forces of the different social systems? We must try to find a more rational and beneficial form of motion for the inevitable contradictions. This is a scientific activity that may bring some social benefit.

NOTES

[1] There is ample literature available on the Hungarian reform. Attention should be drawn particularly to *Nyers* [67], *Friss* (ed.) [33], *Gadó* (ed.) [35], *Gadó* [34] and *Csikós Nagy* [17].

[2] Economic scientists have yet to establish an unambiguous interpretation of the expression "efficiency". Here it is not necessary to become embroiled in the debates surrounding precise definition of it. It will suffice if the reader clearly senses the associations of ideas connected with the concept: we term efficient an activity that makes good uses of the resources and is based on a consideration of the benefits and the sacrifices made to achieve it.

[3] The classical formulation of the principle was given by *Marx* [61] in his *Kritik des Gothaer Programms*.

[4] See *Lange* [56].

[5] Many studies have touched on the problems of the harmonization of and contradictions between economic interests, productivity and ethical requirements in the debate on the reform of the economic mechanism, among them articles by *Hegedűs* [42], *Huszár* [44] and *Berend T.* [12].

[6] In regard to the softening of the budget constraint, and its effect on behaviour of the firm, see the second study in this book.

[7] For a discussion of responsibility for decision-making in investment allocation after the Hungarian reform, see the study by *Deák* [19].

[8] This problem is dealt with in more detail in the following study.

[9] The problems raised in my paper show a certain similarity to the questions of Arrow's celebrated "impossibility theorem". See *Arrow* [3]. Arrow's two postulates are "rationality" desiderata, and two further postulates are "politico-ethical" ones. But Arrow's four postulates and the 5 plus 4 desiderata I have listed are only partly overlapping. Arrow proves with logical rigour the impossibility of the perfect compatibility of his four postulates. I undertake much less: I use only illustrative examples to show the inevitable conflicts of the two different sets of values. I suspect that we could go further than that. It seems to be possible to analyse the contradictions that I have just referred to in a more rigorous, axiomatic form.

The Health of Nations
Reflections on the Analogy between the Medical Sciences and Economics*

Introduction

This essay is built upon an analogy. I examine the similarities between medical science's fighting for the health of the human organism and economics' striving for the health of nations, for the good functioning of economic systems.[1] I deal exclusively with the analogy between the two *disciplines*, and compare the researcher physician to the researcher economist. However interesting it would be, I do not discuss in detail the similarities between the general practitioner's treating the patient and the economic politician and manager's controlling the economic system.

Although the analogy almost tempts to irony and witticism, I should like to refrain from them. I am an economist; and I put the question to myself and my colleagues, "*What can we learn* from another discipline?" We have every reason to look at medical science with due modesty and respect. It has a past of many centuries; ours is only two or three hundred years old. Mankind spends incomparably more intellectual capacity, labour, material means and technical equipment on medical science than it does on economics.

Perhaps the most important difference between the two disciplines is that, in medical science, the relationship between research and its "object", the suffering man wishing to recover, is more immediate than in our trade. Success and failure are much more obvious. The

* First journal publication in English: "The Health of Nations: Reflections on the Analogy between the Medical Sciences and Economics", Kyklos, *Vol. 36 (1983), pp. 191–212. The essay was originally delivered as the acceptance paper of the author receiving the Frank A. Seidman Distinguished Award in Political Economy at Memphis, Tennessee, USA, on September 23, 1982.*

pain and death caused by illness, or the relief of the pain, its elimination and the postponement of death, are alternatives which make the struggle of medical science dramatic. This direct and dramatic nature of the consequences of medical work is a strong propelling force. The gratitude of the patients and their relatives, or, on the contrary, their despair and disillusion, exert great social control and pressure. The impact of the successes and failures of economics is much more indirect and much less spectacular. There is also another important difference. Medical science, like many other natural sciences, can experimentally test most of its hypotheses, whereas economics is deprived of this possibility, apart from some of its narrower fields of examination.

These differences cannot be explained by the personal qualities of the staff of researchers of the two disciplines. Rather, the explanation lies in the objective differences between their positions. Medical science is more mature than economics. This is true even though medicine cannot yet answer many great, vitally important, questions. I do not idealize the present state of medicine; but even with all its shortcomings, it has come much further than our own discipline. It is thus worthwhile to reflect on what we can learn from its philosophy, research methodology and the manner in which it approaches the problems.

I would not like to overshoot the target; far be it from me to develop some kind of "bio-economics". The essential differences between the objects of the two disciplines, and, in consequence, between their methodologies, are obvious. No discipline can base its approach on analogies, on the mechanical adoption of the experiences of other branches of science. But the danger that an analogy driven to the extreme might lead to foolish conclusions should not deter us from trying to analyse, with due caution, the analogy between the two disciplines.[2]

Short pathology

Let us start the line of reasoning with a short *economic pathology*. I should like to keep this survey within narrow limits. I do not undertake to evaluate the economic history of thousands of years, to list and classify all sufferings and agony that accompanied mankind on its way to accumulating material welfare, to developing technologies and organization. Let us restrict ourselves to the present. Even considering this age, I should like to deal exclusively with the diseases of the medium and highly developed economies. The developing countries are struggling with partly similar, partly different maladies; and these will not be dealt with here.

I will list seven *main groups of diseases*. The grouping is arbitrary. I apply several *criteria of classification*, as is done in medicine. There, individual concrete diseases are included in a common main group because they may be traced back to identical or similar causes (e.g. bacterial infections). Or the criterion of grouping is the organ the disease attacks: the heart, the gastrointestinal system and so forth. Other groupings are based on similarities in the course of the sickness or its symptoms, or its consequences. For example, the various kinds of malignant tumours may be classified in a common group of diseases, although their causes are not uniform and they may attack several different organs.

Another arbitrary element of the classification is what we consider as *main* groups of diseases. Many other grave illnesses of the economy are known. But this much is certain, the diseases listed below are considered to be grave by both experts and the majority of laymen. Precisely because they are well-known phenomena, I need not review at length any group of diseases. Almost their mere name is enough to know what kind of trouble of the economic system we have in mind.

1. *Inflation.* Its mild form is the slow, creeping inflation. Its graver form is the galloping inflation. Its fatal form is the ever-accelerating, rushing hyper-inflation. There is no unique, obvious frontier where the "healthy" rise in the price level (perhaps an unavoidable necessity for flexible price movements) ends and the inflationary "disease" begins. The delimitation comprises value judgements, economic policy evaluation. And this is true not only in this case, but also with the other six main groups of diseases as well. This much is, however, certain: every main disease has a degree of intensity which would be classified without hesitation as a deviancy, a functional disturbance, a "disease" by a large part of the experts.

2. *Unemployment*. In mild form it is present in every system. Because of the frictions in the information and decision processes of the labour market, the existing demand and supply do not meet. But the graver forms of unemployment undoubtedly count as diseases; they cause material harm, put the unemployed in a humiliating situation, undermine the feeling of security of those still employed, and cause economic losses to the economic system as a whole. Large unemployment is usually accompanied by a partial underutilization of other material resources: superfluous stocks accumulate, the fixed capital is not fully utilized, and so on.

3. *Shortage*. In this disease, supply regularly lags behind demand. The buyer—a household, an enterprise or a public agency—does not get the desired commodity or service and is forced either to substitute for it something worse or more expensive, or to delay the purchase or give it up altogether. The usual accompanying phenomena are queueing, black markets, corruption, and the indifference of the producer and the seller towards the quality of the product and satisfying the needs of the buyer.

4. *Excessive growth of foreign debts*. To incur a foreign debt is not bad in itself if it is well used. We may speak about a disease if the credits are not adequately used and the country drifts—through a self-generating process—ever deeper into indebtedness. A milder form of the disease is the burden of heavy debt service with which exports cannot keep pace. Its fatal form occurs when the country becomes insolvent.

5. *Growth disturbances*. This is a broad group of diseases with many types. One of the types is abnormally slow growth or stagnation, or even a decline of production and consumption. The opposite type is overambitious, forced growth. A particular mixed case, accompanying mainly the second type, is disproportionate, disharmonious growth. The development of some sector runs ahead, while others degenerate and stagnate, or even get into a catastrophic situation. We may classify the cramps of economic processes among the disturbances of growth into partial crises versus those extending over the whole economy, and periodic accelerations and decelerations.

6. *Inequitable distributions*. A certain inequality in the distribution of income and wealth, and therefore in the consumption of goods and services, is not only compatible with the healthy functioning of the

economy, it is even its condition. It is debated where the necessary, healthy inequality ends and where the degeneration starts: degeneration into inequality of an extent and type that hurts the sense of justice of a large part of the population and hinders the functioning of the economy. But even if this is debated, almost everyone agrees that extravagance and pauperdom live side by side in many kinds of economic systems. There are quite a few who, on account of their individual fate owing to their origin, the colour of their skin, their family situation, health, age or other reasons, live in unjustly disadvantageous situation, while others receive excessive income without merit or performance.

7. *Bureaucratization.* This comes to expression in the fact that an ever-increasing number of *allocative and distributive decisions* pass from the hands of the directly affected, materially and morally directly interested persons, into the scope of the impersonal authority of the apparatus of large offices and organizations. Simultaneously, dependency relationships come about. Those personally affected, afflicted or raised by the allocative and distributive decision get into a position of depending on the bureaucracy. The disease becomes particularly dangerous if a cancer-like proliferation appears and the cells of bureaucracy start to divide irresistibly, squeezing out the healthy tissue.

It may be stated that *we cannot find a single country among the medium and highly developed ones that would be completely free from each of the above seven main diseases*. The situation of a country may be said to be relatively favourable if it is tormented only by a single main disease and this is complemented at most by two or three other ones in some milder form. The situation is worse in many economies; they are gravely hit by two or three or even more diseases and to a lesser extent by quite a few other ones as well.

This situation causes difficulties in defining the "health" status of economic systems. For the medical science, health is a basic concept that can only be explained by circumscription, tautologically. The human organism is healthy if its every organ functions well and adjusts to changes well.[3] Description of the healthy organism is made easier by the fact that its characteristics can be empirically observed and measured. According to the rules of representative sampling, a large number of healthy people can be observed and the distribution of the most important parameters of, for example, their heart action, can be taken into account. Finally, a statistical inference can be drawn from the fact that the heart of a healthy man in a state of rest beats at a rate of 60–80 per minute in an even rhythm. Those whose hearts beat more quickly or arrhythmically are, presumably, not healthy. The statistical description of the healthy heart-beat becomes the more unambiguous the more we succeed in excluding from the sample those who suffer from either heart disease or any other disease; that is, only the heart action parameters of people qualified as healthy are registered in order to empirically delimit the healthy domain of the parameters. Every concrete statement of anatomy and physiology about the characteristic properties of the healthy human organism relies on the premise that there *exist* healthy people whose *entire* organism, not just one or another organ, is healthy. It was not given to economics to base the concept of "health" on a similar premise and on the empirical statistical observation of healthy systems. Since history has to this very day not created an economy that is healthy in every respect, for our discipline, "health" is merely a *hypothetical* category. We only have a *partial* empirical background. If, for example, we consider the economy lastingly free from unemployment as healthy, we can only refer to such existing—not hypothetical, but empirically observable—economic system, which, though having eliminated unemployment, are plagued by other grave diseases such as shortage, bureaucratization, etc. The perfectly healthy economy is thus an *idealization* which puts together the model of a complete system from the, in themselves, healthy subsystems of different existing real systems.[4]

The picture of a completely healthy economy can only be drawn in the framework of normative theory. For example, a theory can be worked out in axiomatic form which derives from definite ethical and political postulates, desiderata, what properties a system should have to satisfy these postulates. In this essay I do not undertake such a theoretical analysis. It seems sufficient for my reasoning if I approach the problem in a pragmatic manner. Those processes are considered to be "diseases" of the economic system if (1) they cause direct or indirect physical and mental suffering to many members of the system, and economic losses to the whole of society, and (2) they can be shown not to appear in some economic system of the present. Therefore, in accordance with the second condition, in this essay the processes involving losses and suffering which are present in our day *in every system and at every time,* without exception, are not considered to be "diseases".[5]

The question might now be raised: how big is the role of the study of diseases in the two disciplines to be compared? Let us first consider medicine. If we think only of the literature now used throughout the world and neglect the older works, hundreds of general textbooks on pathology are in circulation; and the number of partial pathological works certainly runs into thousands, if not more. Medical students, at the beginning of their studies, learn at least as much about the anatomy and physiology of the sick organism as about those of the healthy one. Then, in the individual clinical subjects, the proportions are similar when an organ or a system is treated.

As against that, in economic research and education the proportions in the examination of "health" and "disease" are quite different. If we examine any one of the comprehensive American textbooks on economics we discover that most of the material is devoted to how the economy would function if it functioned well. "Pathology" hardly features. The situation is similar with the textbooks from which the political economy of socialism is taught at the East European universities of economics. In these books too, there are, at most, a few pages devoted to the characteristic illnesses of the economy.

True, there are economic researchers in both West and East who specialize in the analysis of one or another illness. There are diseases which are discussed in a huge literature (e.g. inflation or unemployment). Important works were published about a few other evils (e.g. unequal distribution of income), but they are less in the focus of interest. And, finally, there are also maladies which have hardly been studied as yet (e.g. bureaucratization or shortage).[6] And what is most characteristic of the state of our discipline in this respect is that there is no single economic work that *comprehensively* discusses the diseases of economic systems.[7] As a matter of fact, their mere systematization, classification and a methodological summary of the causes, symptoms and consequences would be highly instructive.

Effect and side-effect

One of the basic problems of medical treatment is to weigh the desired effects and the adverse side-effects of the therapy. Be it medicinal treatment, or surgical intervention, or any other kind of therapy, the desired main effects are accompanied by adverse side-effects. Let us consider the example of the corticosteroids. These are hormonal preparations which are applied in the case of many illnesses. They are used for treating asthma, arthritis, dermatitis and many other diseases. The patient sometimes feels it is a panacea; in long-lasting pathologic processes a quick improvement ensues and tormenting pains cease in a short time. He would like to persuade his doctors to use the preparation not only temporarily, but for some longer time. Yet the side-effects are as strong as the main effects. In cases in which the corticosteroid preparations are taken for a longer time, they might disturb the functioning of the hormonal system, the sugar metabolism, the salt and water household, the skeletal system, etc. The physician has to reflect with great circumspection upon, and consult with the patient about, what kind of side-effect the desired main effect is worth incurring.

Treatment with the corticosteroids is a particularly sharp, but not a unique, example. Perhaps in less extreme form, a similar problem emerges with every kind of therapy. The opinion is widespread among physicians that no true effect can be hoped for from a medicament which has no side-effect.

A physician friend of mine handed me one of the standard books of the huge literature on side-effects: *Meyler's Side Effects of Drugs— An Encyclopaedia of Adverse Reactions and Interactions.*[8] The work has reached its ninth edition and the international editorial board continually rewrites it using the latest scientific achievements. For me, an economist by profession, even the structure of the volume has been highly instructive. It reviews the field by groups of medicaments and classifies the information with each group of medicaments according to the following subtitles:

(i) *Adverse reaction pattern*. The adverse side-effects are summed up here.

(ii) *Organs and systems*. This section examines in turn all parts, starting with the cardiovascular system and the respiratory system, through the liver and the kidney, and ending with the skin, and presents in detail all side-effects of the drug in question on these organs and systems.

(iii) *Risk situations*. The drug might, perhaps, be given to a patient who in addition to the disease for which the drug is intended also suffers from another disease or from another anomaly, or with whom age (infant, child, aged) or pregnancy might cause additional problems. In considering the side-effects, particular attention has to be paid to these various risk situations.

(iv) *Interaction*. What is the effect of the drug in question if it is administered along with other drugs?

In connection with each statement the book gives short information about the expected frequency of the side-effect and the sound foundations of the observation. It also raises such problems of side-effects which have not yet been satisfactorily clarified, but also points to the necessity of further investigations.

I turned the pages of the book with no small embarrassment in the name of my profession. How far we are from having systematically collected the adverse side-effects of therapies!

And now let us pass to the main diseases of economic systems. For the time being, I shall discuss the scope of problems treated in the said encyclopaedia under (i) and (ii), that is, the primary problems of the interrelations between effect and side-effect. We shall later return to the subjects of risk situation and interaction.

Let us take in turn the seven main diseases of the medium and highly developed economic systems of our day, for the treatment of which economists suggest various therapies. (The figures in parentheses indicate the serial numbers of the diseases emerging as side-effects.)[9]

Main disease No. 1: inflation. Inflation may be slowed down or eliminated with one of several instruments, or perhaps with the combined application of various instruments. If the main instrument of the therapy is restriction of the money supply or of public expenditures, that is, in the final analysis, a restriction of demand, then the typical side-effects are declining production (5) and increasing unemployment (2). The present state of the USA and several other developed capitalist economies shows well this interrelation. And if, for the purposes of anti-inflationary therapy, the administrative control of prices and wages is applied with great force, then the usual side-effect is the disturbance of the regular course of market processes, the proliferation of bureaucracy (7). This is perhaps also accompanied by shortage phenomena (3). In such cases in a capitalist economy repressed inflation takes the place of open inflation; and with it the usual symptoms appear: bottleneck, queueing, forced substitution caused by shortage, the black and the grey market.

Main disease No. 2: unemployment. Let us first look at the capitalist economy. The main side-effect of the Keynesian measures applied to fight unemployment is, as has been stated a hundred times in recent years, the acceleration of inflation (1). As regards the socialist economy, it is capable permanently of eliminating unemployment; in fact, the labour market shifts into a state of chronic labour shortage. This is guaranteed by the operating mechanism of the economy, by the interests of the decision-makers, and by the growth strategy of economic policy which creates an incessant expansion drive, investment hunger and an almost unlimited demand for production inputs. All that absorbs the previously unused resources, including massive unemployment. At the same time, however, these processes are in every case accompanied by the side-effects of chronic shortages (3), the bureaucratization of economic processes (7) and, if not in every case, yet in rather many cases, by an excessive increase, and perhaps even an accelerating increase, of foreign indebtedness (4). We can witness this in several East European countries.

Main disease No. 3: shortage. For a long time it was Yugoslavia that supplied the most illustrative example of the side-effect of reforms aimed at fighting the shortage economy. They allowed a wider role to the market and the price mechanism. In its wake, unsatisfied demand, queueing and the black market ceased in a wide scope. But, together with this, there emerged inflation (1), which, at times, accelerated rapidly. There is considerable unemployment (2) in the country, which is partly open and partly hidden because the excess supply of labour is drained by the export of guest-workers to the developed European capitalist countries. Foreign indebtedness is excessive (4).

In Hungary, too, similar problems emerge, if in less distinct form. In some sectors of the economy successes were achieved in fighting chronic shortages. Partly as a side-effect and partly under the impact of other factors, several other difficulties have emerged. Among others, the inflationary tendency gathered momentum (1) and the stock of debts has grown rapidly (4). We shall return to the problems of Hungary in the context of disease No. 7.

Main disease No. 4: excessive growth of foreign indebtedness. This disease is spreading in our day like a plague, hardly any country is free from it. It is treated with several therapies, by devaluing the national currency, protectionistic tariff policy, the administrative restriction of imports, export subsidies, etc. Several side-effects appear: a slowing down of growth or perhaps an absolute decline of output (5) and as a symptom accompanying the latter, the growth of unemployment in the West (2), or the increase of domestic shortage phenomena in Eastern Europe (3). The therapy frequently leads to the acceleration of inflation (1). Insofar as administrative measures are resorted to either for restricting imports or for the forced securing of exports, this entails the bureaucratization of certain economic processes (7).

Main disease No. 5: growth disturbances. As an example I cite here merely the typical growth disturbance in the capitalist countries, cyclical fluctuation, and within that, particularly the phases of recession. Their therapy is linked to the treatment of unemployment. Accordingly, the side-effects are also similar. The most important among these is the acceleration of inflation (1).

Main disease No. 6: inequitable distribution. In the capitalist world it was the Scandinavian countries that started most energetically to cure this grave illness, first of all by means of heavy and steeply progressive taxation, with the free or almost free provision of several services (education, health service, etc.), and then with extensive insurance against sickness, disability, old age and unemployment. While in these countries great progress was made towards equality and economic security, several adverse side-effects have appeared. Part of the economic processes has become bureaucratic (7), shortages emerged in some subsidized services (3), the expansion of public services put a heavy burden on the state budget whose deficit contributed to accelerating inflation (1). In addition, other negative consequences emerged (e.g. the weakening of incentives for work performance) which have not even been listed among the major diseases.

Main disease No. 7: bureaucratization. Its main therapy is deregulation, the handing over of control by administrative institutions to control through the market mechanism. We can observe this therapy in several developed capitalist countries such as the USA, Britain, etc. And even if the starting-point is essentially different, the direction of change is similar in the reforms of some East European countries, among them Hungary. Several kinds of side-effects appear. Since some of the redistributive bureaucratic regulations served egalitarian-levelling purposes, removal of these regulations leads to increasing inequalities in incomes and wealth (6). A similar effect is entailed by the liquidation or reduction of state subsidies previously given to enterprises and social groups or strata. This will obviously deteriorate the material living standards and economic security of those affected, and increase the income differences between enterprises earning profits and those incurring losses. A further characteristic side-effect is that the elimination of the bureaucratic regulation of prices and wages allows a freer way for the, up to then, repressed inflation (1).

We have reached the end of our list. The space available for the essay does not allow dwelling on any trade-off. While I could indicate very grave problems with but one or two sentences, this brief survey leads to sufficiently depressing conclusions. It seems reality does not even pose the question how an economy, healthy in every respect, can be attained. It is possible that the real decision dilemma facing countries, peoples, parties, governments, statesmen and, ultimately, citizens, is: which kind of disease do you choose if perfect health is unattainable?

Is this conclusion not too pessimistic? I wish from the bottom of my heart that science could refute this statement. The proof or the refutation can be made in one of two ways. The first is a *theoretical* investigation of the trade-offs between the diseases of economic systems. I am afraid that the more carefully and circumspectly the model-builder takes into account every effect of some therapy, the nearer he will come to the above reasoning, according to which, for radical cures, we pay with new and grave ills. Unfortunately, theoretical literature discusses the interrelations between two, at most three, main diseases. A comprehensive theoretical analysis devoted to investigating, methodically and in full depth, the interrelations among the seven main diseases listed by me, and even further side-effects, has not yet been done.

The argument is decided far more by the study of *historical experience* than by a purely theoretical examination. I venture the following proposition: *In the course of history, whenever an advanced stage of some main economic disease came to prevail in an economic system, and a radical therapy was started, at least one other main disease developed to a conspicuous extent.*

I would call attention to the restrictions on the above proposition. I speak only about those cases in which some main disease already plagues one or another system in a *grave* form and the therapy used for fighting it is *radical*. Mild treatment of a slight illness does not necessarily entail these inevitable shifts from one great trouble to another one.

It does *not* follow from my line of reasoning that one must never undertake radical treatment or that it is never worthwhile to do so. Medical science proposes in several cases definitely grave surgical intervention, strong drugs, or radio-therapy, although it knows only too well that these involve perhaps serious adverse side-effects. But it can only do so if it weighs the ensemble of the remedial and harmful effects of the therapy with circumspection and finds that the expectable advantage is worth the disadvantages.[10] It has to share the responsibility for decisions with the patient or, if he is in a state incapable of decision, with his relative. Let us sincerely confess: this kind of approach is not infrequently missing from the advocates of the revolutionary transformation or radical reform of economic systems. They usually emphasize exclusively that in the prevailing situation this or that disease is unsupportably tormenting society, that unemployment or inflation, the injustice of distribution, or bureaucracy, are intolerable. The "patient", society or at least a considerable part of society, deeply feels the sufferings caused by the evil in question and agrees with the proposed radical changes. The mistake is made when the scientist proposing the therapy does not disclose (i.e. he suppresses, or perhaps has himself not thought it through sufficiently) that although the turn eliminates the hitherto pressing evil, it might perhaps cause the appearance of new diseases.[11]

It may happen that the majority of society would accept the proposed therapy even if it knew the expected adverse side-effects. (The patient, too, always wishes most urgently to recover from that disease which torments him most at the moment.) But it also might happen that society would rather put up with the well-known old trouble than suffer from a new one. The choice of the radical therapy and the accompanying adverse side-effects is, in the final analysis, a decision which implies a value judgement, a political and ethical choice.

Risk situation and interaction

Let us return to the chapters of the encyclopaedia of side-effects, to the items (iii) and (iv) not yet treated. Let us first consider item (iii), the problem called by the physician a *risk situation*. The same medicament that can be taken without fear by an otherwise healthy man might cause grave troubles for someone who is suffering from, e.g., some disease of the liver or the kidney. The operation which a surgeon safely carries out on a young or middle-aged patient, will not be undertaken with an aged one.

Many economists are less cautious and give less consideration to the concrete situation of the patient. They bravely propose their cherished recipes, without weighing carefully what the particular situation of the economy in question is and how it is economically, socially and politically endangered. Characteristic examples of this approach are the most rigid, most orthodox exponents of the monetarist school. They propose the same recipe for the USA, Britain, Chile, Israel, and even for China, Yugoslavia and Hungary, irrespective of the huge differences among the economic development levels, social systems and political structures of these countries, and irrespective of the attitude of the government, the employers and employees, the state bureaucracy and the trade unions, to the monetarist policy.[12] The same economic policy that serves well in some country in a definite historical situation, may fail in another country or lead to the sharpening of the internal social conflicts of the system. Or it may be that it simply cannot be implemented because of the resistance of society. Just as the co-operation of the patient is needed in curing his own disease, in the same manner, or even more so, the support of the population is needed in curing the diseases of the economic system.

I would like to illustrate problem (iv) listed in the encyclopaedia of side-effects, the economic analogy of *interaction* among the drugs, by means of experiences in Hungary in the last one and a half decades.

For a long time economic policy was used in an attempt to combat two troubles simultaneously: the weakness of economic stimulation and the injustice of social distribution. The medicaments of the former were the introduction of the profit motive in state enterprises and permitting private ventures in several fields. The medicaments of the second evil were wage policy and taxation measures promoting the levelling of incomes. But these are drugs which mutually deteriorate each other's effect. The many kinds of egalitarian measures, the guaranteeing of the survival of enterprises and the maintenance of every job blunt the stimulating power of profit. Some stronger interference with the distribution of income may deter private initiative from pursuing a long-term business policy and making major investments. At the same time, the introduction of market relations, the profit motive and private initiative was enough to increase the inequalities in the distribution of income and wealth and thus hurt the sense of justice of many people.

The origin and endurance of the diseases

Medical science classifies the diseases from several points of view. It is worthwhile to reflect on some of these points of view for the sake of the economic analogy.

One of the important distinctions is whether we have to deal with a *congenital* disease or with some disorder *contracted* in the course of life. Part of the former is not considered a disease in medicine; rather, it is qualified as an anomaly. These are the cases of deviation from the normal, from the healthy, with which the human organism in question lives throughout his life.

Insofar as a congenital trouble is faced, the question arises: is it an *inherited* disease or has the anomaly resulted from effects suffered during the embryonic period or birth, or from other causes?

In many cases, because of inheritance or for some other reason, the individual was not born ill, but has a congenital *predisposition* to some definite illnesses. He whose parents were both diabetic has a greater likelihood of contracting diabetes. The illness may then break out with growing age, or under the impact of other circumstances, e.g. faulty nutritional habits.

A further important distinction: is it an *acute* disease of which the patient may be unambiguously cured with the aid of his own internal defensive mechanisms and eventual medical interference, or is it a *chronic* malady from which the patient cannot completely recover in the remaining part of his life? In the latter case, the gravity of the illness might still be influenced through a proper way of life and medical treatment, and therefore we might ask: will the disease deteriorate rapidly or can the deterioration be slowed down? Or even: can the state of the patient be perhaps substantially improved? In any case, the chronic illness requires constant attention, adjustment and careful treatment.

In some cases the acute form of some contracted disease may be fought, but a *predisposition to the renewal of the illness* persists. It is well known, e.g., that the skin of someone who once contracts a fungal infection will be inclined to new infection even after it is healed. True, in such cases the predisposition is insufficient for the outbreak of the disease. The primary cause of the new infection, in our case re-exposure to the fungi, is absolutely necessary. But fungi which cause infection of the skin are found in great abundance in many places. It is thus a question of primary importance to what extent one or another individual is predisposed to infection.

And now let us return to economics. The main weakness of economic pathology consists in the fact that it does not delimit the various maladies adequately according to the above classification. Is inflation some acute contracted disease caused by external "infections"? This kind of causal explanation may be found behind the theory of "imported inflation". Or is it the truth that a modern economy, particularly in its periods of rapid growth, has a congenital inclination to chronic inflation? Is massive unemployment caused exclusively by the anti-inflationary policy of conservative governments or is it a congenital anomaly of the capitalist economic system? Or, in other words, is it perhaps a malady which can be eliminated for some longer time only by means of artificial stimulation, which, however, "over-stimulates" the blood circulation and nervous system and leads to inflation, grave indebtedness and other negative consequences? Are the shortage phenomena merely *ad hoc* disturbances in the socialist economy, or is this, too, a congenital anomaly of highly centralized and bureaucratic economic managament?

The physician has to face the phenomena of congenital anomaly, inherited malady, chronic illness and predisposition to some definite disease. Just because he wishes to cure, or at least to alleviate, the trouble and the pain, he must not brush aside the idea of the chronic nature of some disease; and he does not have the right to comfort himself or the patient by claiming that it is merely a passing and easily healed problem. Let us confess that the economist, precisely because of the political and ideological nature of his profession, frequently gives a biased and distorted picture of the problem. Though he believes of the patient of *another* doctor that his illness, or at least his predisposition to the illness, is congenital, or that the contracted anomaly is chronic, he comforts *his own* patient and himself by saying that the patient will soon recover if he accepts his recipe and the treatment.

Some professional and ethical conclusions

From what has been said a few more general conclusions follow. Some are of a professional nature in the closer sense, others are related to the ethical problems of scientific research.

We usually distinguish between positive and normative economic analysis. With some simplification one might say that the first examines what *exists,* the latter what *should be.* I must confess that as long as I have been engaged in economic research, I have felt again and again some suspicion, and frequently even aversion, to most of the normative theories. Now, having reflected about the analogy between medicine and economics, I better understand my own suspicion and aversion. A large part of the normative theories in economics—and the bulk of the theories based on the most diverse ideologies and political faiths may be classified here—tries to outline the *ideal* economic system or its individual parts. In the medical science, too, there exist both positive and normative analyses. But these are separated from and linked to each other in a different manner. Anatomy and physiology describe the structure and functioning of the healthy human organism, but those of the actually existing man, and not of some ideally perfect one. The human organism is a marvellous machine, but it is far from perfect; it is full of clumsy and fragile elements. It is a good thing that we have reserves of a few important organs. We have two eyes, two ears, two lungs. It is a pity that we do not have two hearts. But a reasonable physician does not ask whether or not this is an ideal state of affairs, whether an optimal human organism should not possess even two hearts. The human organism is such as it is, and we have to set out from this fact and not from some phantasm of perfection.[13] It is also a part of positive reality that people may be tormented by a thousand kinds of disease. Therefore, *the intelligent posing of the normative problem does not set out from the ideal state, but from the reality of the disease. How can some concrete disease be cured; or, if this is impossible, how can its course and its consequences be alleviated?* Although this formulation of problems is not unknown in our profession, it is mostly not in the focus of research and education.

The normative theories of economics are deeply interwoven with a *naïve optimism*. According to one normative theory, the individual makes decisions that are optimal for his own self-interest. The advocates of this normative theory, trusting the perfection of the market, add that if we allow the market, and only the market, to harmonize the atomized individual decision-makers, the functioning of the national economy as a whole will be equally optimal. The protagonists of the normative theory based on a belief in the almightiness of planning, however, reach the no less optimistic conclusion that the foresight of planners is capable of optimally co-ordinating the activities of every member of society.

Sometimes an exceptional scholar appears, one who has the courage to state that there exist *insoluble* dilemmas. Although today belittled by many, in my opinion Phillips has earned great merit. True, according to the present state of macro-economics, the Phillips curve requires much complementing for precision; and it only partially shows the interaction between unemployment and inflation. But even so, Phillips belongs among the first ones who sharply exposed the deep dilemma referred to in the present study as the general scope of problems of effect and side-effect. Another classic example is Arrow's work on social choice. Arrow pointed out that it is impossible to satisfy simultaneously every desirable and rational postulate of social choice.[14] Some of the postulates will be unavoidably infringed upon. A third example is Lindbeck's argument that it is naïvety to long for an economic system in which there is neither the market, with its particular negative social consequences, nor bureaucracy, with its other kind of harmful social side-effects.[15] But even if there are such works, it is not these that give the basic tone to our profession; instead, the tone is the blind optimism of Voltaire's Doctor Pangloss.

Medicine is, in a sense, "pessimistic" because it boldly faces the fact that the overwhelming majority of people will sometimes fall ill in the course of their lives, perhaps even several times, and usually die, in the end, from some disease. But this pessimism does not hold it back from action; in fact, this is what prompts it to scientific research and to the application of the achievements of science. This is staggeringly expressed by the physician hero of Camus's *The Plague,* Rieux, in his conversation with his friend, Tarrou, who helps him in fighting the plague. "Oui, approuva Tarrou, je peux comprendre. Mais vos victoires seront toujours provisoires, voilà tout." — Rieux parut s'assombrir. — "Toujours, je le sais. Ce n'est pas une raison pour cesser de lutter."[16]

It is foreign to medical science and to its responsible and ethical application to act at any price, irrespective of the consequences, but no less foreign is passivity, reliance on faith that everything has to be left to nature which will cure every malady by itself. The economic protagonists of the latter view in the West are those who proclaim that the market will solve every problem in due course if only it is not disturbed by government interventions. Even if there are troubles, let the natural forces of the market overcome them. There also exists a symmetrical statement in the East: If there are problems, let planning solve them one by one. There is no such evil that would require a reform, a deeper interference with the structure of society. We must not accept such conservative inertia. We must fight with the forces we have for healing the diseases of society.

The faith and the illusion of the strictly rational man, the perfect market, the perfect planning, or the optimal social system are not necessary for economics to do honest work. The world economy is in a dismal state. There is no reason for us to believe that in the near future everything will turn for the better. I think that the economist researcher of the late twentieth century has every reason for anxiety, desperation and anger. But this should not reduce him to inactivity and capitulation. The state of the world economy, and of our own discipline, should at least prompt us to exhibit due modesty, to refrain from the cocksureness of the fanatical quacks, and to sincerely confess to the limits of our knowledge. We must take a stand in the name of our science more cautiously, more considerately, more circumspectly, when giving advice in matters relating to the healing of the sick economy.

NOTES

[1] The English title "The Health of Nations" recalls, of course, the title of Adam Smith's classic work, *The Wealth of Nations,* an allusion untranslatable, for instance, into Hungarian.

Thanks are due to the physicians Dr. Tibor Fazekas, Dr. Hedvig Graber and Dr. Árpád Székely for their valuable advice. My study has been inspired by several works; I should like to mention especially the volume *Diagnózisok* [Diagnoses] by Elemér *Hankiss,* an eminent Hungarian sociologist and social philosopher [40].

[2] Several economists have noticed the importance of biological analogies; among others are Marshall, Boulding and Georgescu-Roegen. See the article by *Thoben* [81].

[3] The constitution of the World Health Organization of the United Nations [84] laid down the following palpable (though, as a matter of fact, similarly tautological) definition: health is a state of complete physical, mental and social well-being. On the concept of health, see also *Simonovits* [72].

[4] It is food for thought that the Hungarian language has no independent noun corresponding to "health". The Hungarian noun *(egészség)* is formed from the adjective *"whole" (egész)* and thus it literally means something like "being whole" or "complete".

[5] Other definitions of the health and disease of economic systems are also conceivable. For example, in other works of mine I, too, interpreted the "normal state" of economic systems in a different manner. In this essay,

however, for the whole line of reasoning which relies on the analogy to medicine, the above definition seems to be the most appropriate one.

[6] It is, rather, sociologists who discuss bureaucratization. (See, e.g., the works of Merton, Crozier, Gouldner and, from among the Hungarian ones, those of Hegedűs and Kulcsár.) Although the problem frequently emerges in economic works as a side-issue, to my knowledge no major *economic* work has been published as yet which has chosen the bureaucratization of economic process for its main subject.

It was the author of the present lines who wrote the first monograph about the chronic shortage appearing in the socialist economy [51].

[7] Sociology already has a few general works on social pathology. See, e.g., B. *Wooton*'s book [85]. For the interest of sociology in pathology see *Hankiss* [40].

[8] Excerpta Medica, Amsterdam, 1980.

[9] I illustrate my message at times with examples taken from the capitalist system, at times with those from the socialist system, and at times from both systems. For reasons of space restrictions I cannot touch in every case on the problems of both systems.

[10] Medical science and practice, for a long time, regarded the principle of *nil nocere* (do not harm) as an ethical postulate. Modern medicine has recognized that the application of this principle is wrong since it would restrict the opportunities for healing. In its present approach it weighs the benefit-risk ratio and the benefit-cost ratio. To this extent it has then come nearer to the rationally calculating approach of decision theory and normative economics.

[11] This kind of neglect was committed by Marxist social scientists, when, seeing the evils caused by the market, they did not analyse what new and different troubles may be caused by the elimination of the market. Or, when the Keynesians, proposing the well-known therapy for the troubles caused by unemployment, did not thoroughly reflect on the dangers involved in inflation and bureaucratization accompanying government interference.

[12] Although in the Introduction I promised to refrain from irony, I cannot resist here recalling the physician's examination from Molière's *Le malade imaginaire*. The candidate is examined in turn by the learned doctors, how he would cure oedema, colic, asthma, the disease of the spleen or of the lungs, and so forth. The candidate answers the same, word for word, to every question in Latin: "Clisterium donare—Postea seignare—Ensuitta purgare." (In rough translation: "First irrigation, then venesection, ultimately purgation.") This monotonous answer is sufficient for being admitted to the learned order of physicians.

The quotation is from Molière's *Œuvres Complètes*. Vol. 8, Société des Belles Lettres, Paris 1952, p. 238.

[13] At this point some readers of the manuscript of my essay made sharp objections. They emphasized that the human organism is a creation of nature and thus its biological properties are fundamentally given and can be little changed. As against that, the structure of society is brought about by men and may be changed by men. I acknowledge that; and I would not like to drive the analogy to the extreme at this place, either. Indeed, great thinkers, politicians, mass movements, parties, may have a deep impact on the structure of society. But let me add, precisely in this essay, that their effect may assert itself *within certain limits only*. There are changes which, using a medical term, are capable of "becoming organic", which the society amalgamates deeply and lastingly. And there are artificial, unnatural changes, which society sooner or later eliminates, just as certain transplanted organs are rejected by the immune system of the human organism.

[14] See *Arrow* [3] and [4], pp. 12–15 and 153–155 respectively.

[15] See *Lindbeck* [57].

[16] In rough English translation: "Yes," agreed Tarrou, "I can understand you. But your victories will always be temporary and that is that." Rieux's eyes darkened, "Always, I am clear about that. But this is not reason to abandon the fight."

(The source of the French quotation is this: A. Camus: *La Peste*. Gallimard, Paris, 1947, p. 147.)

References

[1] ANGELUSZ, R.–PATAKI, J.: *A jövedelemkülönbségek alakulásának tükröződése a közvéleményben* [Reflection of Income Differentials in Public Opinion], mimeo, Budapest, Tömegkommunikációs Központ, 1976.

[2] ANTAL, L.: "Development with Some Digression—The Hungarian Economic Mechanism in the Seventies", *Acta Oeconomica, 23*, 3–4, 257–274, 1979.

[3] ARROW, K. J.: *Social Choice and Individual Values*, New York, Wiley, 1951.

[4] ARROW, K. J.: *Egyensúly és döntés [Equilibrium and Decision]*, Budapest, Közgazdasági és Jogi Könyvkiadó, 1979.

[5] ARROW, K. J.–HAHN, F.: *General Competitive Analysis*, San Francisco, Holden–Day, 1971.

[6] BARRO, R. J.–GROSSMAN, H. I.: "Suppressed Inflation and the Supply Multiplier", *Review of Economic Studies, 41*, 87–104, 1974.

[7] BÁRSONY, J.: "Tibor Liska's Concept, the Socialist Entrepreneurship", *Acta Oeconomica, 28*, 3–4, 422–455, 1982.

[8] BAUER, T.: "Investment Cycles in Planned Economies", *Acta Oeconomica, 21*, 3, 243–260, 1978.

[9] BAUER, T.: *Tervgazdaság, beruházás, ciklusok* [Planned Economy, Investment, Cycles], Budapest, Közgazdasági és Jogi Könyvkiadó, 1981.

[10] BAUER, T.: *A beruházási volumen a közvetlen tervgazdálkodásban* [The Level of Investment in the Centrally Planned Economy], mimeo, Budapest, MTA Közgazdaságtudományi Intézet, 1977.

[11] BAUER, T.: "The Contradictory Position of the Enterprise under the New Hungarian Economic Mechanism", *Coexistence, 13*, 65–80, 1978.

[12] BEREND T., I.: "Ten Years after–Instead of a Balance Sheet", *Acta Oeconomica, 20*, 1–2, 45–60, 1981.

[13] BRÓDY, A.: "A Linearised Model of the Cycle", *Acta Oeconomica, 21*, 3, 261–267, 1978.

[14] BRÓDY, A.: "The Logic of Market Behaviour", *Acta Oeconomica, 14*, 49–58, 1975.

[15] CSANÁDINÉ DEMETER, M.: "A vállalatnagyság, a jövedelmezőség és a preferenciák néhány összefüggése" [Some Interrelations between the Size of the Firm, Profitability and Preferences], *Pénzügyi Szemle*, 2, 105–120, 1979.

[16] CSERESNÉ KOVÁCS, ZS.: "A mezőgazdasági kistermelés termelőerői" [The Production Forces of Small-scale Farming], *Proceedings of the Institute of Economics*, No. 23, 1981.

[17] CSIKÓS-NAGY, B.: "Ten Years of the Hungarian Economic Reform", *New Hungarian Quarterly*, 70, 31–37, 1978.

[18] CSIKÓS-NAGY, B.: "Adalékok az inflációelmélethez" [Contributions to Inflation Theory], *Közgazdasági Szemle*, 22, 564–575, 1975.

[19] DEÁK, A.: "Enterprise Investment Decisions and Economic Efficiency", *Acta Oeconomica*, 20, 1–2, 63–68, 1978.

[20] DEÁK, A.: *Állami pénzügyi befolyásolás, preferenciák és diszpreferenciák* [Central Financial Influence, Preferences and Dispreferences], mimeo, Budapest, Pénzügyminisztérium, 1972.

[21] DEÁK, A. [ed.]: *Pénzügyi megkülönböztetések rendszere* [System of Financial Differentiation], mimeo, Budapest, Pénzügyminisztérium, 1972.

[22] DONÁTH, F.: *Reform and Revolution — Transformation of Hungary's Agriculture 1945–1975*, Budapest, Corvina, 1980.

[23] FÁBRI, E.: "Felszíni változások és mélyen fekvő tendenciák a készletfolyamatokban" [Superficial Changes and Underlying Tendencies in the Processes of Inventories], *Pénzügyi Szemle* 25, 10, 728–739, 1981.

[24] FALUBIRÓ, V.–GÁLIK, L.: "A nyereség részarányok visszarendeződési tendenciájáról" [On the Tendency of Reversion of Profitability], *Pénzügyi Szemle*, 25, 12, 909–915, 1981.

[25] FALUSNÉ SZIKRA, K.: "On Economic Competition", *Acta Oeconomica*, 13, 1, 49–64, 1974.

[26] FALUVÉGI, L.: *Állami pénzügyek és gazdaságirányítás* [State Finances and Economic Control], Budapest, Közgazdasági és Jogi Könyvkiadó, 1977.

[27] FARKAS, K.–PATAKI, J.: *Vélemények néhány aktuális gazdasági kérdésről* [Opinions about Some Topical Economic Problems], mimeo, Budapest, Tömegkommunikációs Központ, 1980.

[28] FENYŐVÁRI, I.: "The Role of Profit in the Hungarian Economy", *Acta Oeconomica*, 22, 1–2, 33–46, 1979.

[29] FRIEDMAN, M.–HAYEK, F. A. et al.: *Inflation: Causes, Consequences, Cures*, London, IEA, 1974.

[30] FRISS, I. [ed.]: *Reform of the Economic Mechanism in Hungary*, Budapest, Akadémiai Kiadó, 1971.

[31] GÁBOR, R. I.: "A második (másodlagos) gazdaság" [The Second (Secondary) Economy], *Valóság*, 22, 1, 22–36, 1979.

[32] Gábor, R. I.–Galasi, P.: A "második"g azdaság [The Second Economy], Budapest, Közgazdasági és Jogi Könyvkiadó, 1981.

[33] Gács, J.: "Hiány és támogatott fejlesztés" [Shortage and Subsidized Development], Közgazdasági Szemle, 23, 1043–1060, 1976.

[34] Gadó, O.: The Economic Mechanism in Hungary, How it Works in 1976, Budapest–Leyden, Akadémiai Kiadó–Sijthoff, 1976.

[35] Gadó, O. [ed.]: Reform of the Economic Mechanism in Hungary, Budapest, Akadémiai Kiadó, 1972.

[36] Galbraith, J. K.: Economics and the Public Purpose, Boston, Houghton–Mifflin, 1973.

[37] Goldmann, J.–Kouba, K.: Economic Growth in Czechoslovakia, Prague, Academia, 1969.

[38] Graaf, J. de V.: Theoretical Welfare Economics, Cambridge, Cambridge University Press, 1957.

[39] Háda, L.–Trautmann, J.: "Koncentráció és gazdaságosság" [Concentration and Efficiency], Pénzügyi Szemle, 24, 197–203, 1980.

[40] Hankiss, E.: Diagnózisok [Diagnoses], Budapest, Magvető Kiadó, 1982.

[41] Hansen, B.: A Study in the Theory of Inflation, London, Allen–Unwin, 1951.

[42] Hegedűs, A.: "Optimalizálás és humanizálás" [Optimization and Humanization], Valóság, 8, 3, 17–32, 1965.

[43] Hirschman, A. O.: Essays in Trespassing, Cambridge, Cambridge UP, 1981.

[44] Huszár, T.: "Gazdaság, érdek, erkölcs" [Economy, Interest, Morale], Valóság, 8, 12, 1–14, 1965.

[45] Kaldor, N.: "The Irrelevance of Equilibrium Economics", Economic Journal, 82, 1237–1255, 1972.

[46] Kalecki, M.: "Theories of Growth in Different Social Systems", Scientia, 40, 1–6, 1970.

[47] Kapitány, Zs.–Kornai, J.–Szabó, J.: "The Reproduction of Shortage on the Hungarian Car Market", Soviet Studies, 36, 236–256, 1983.

[48] Keynes, J. M.: The General Theory of Employment, Interest and Money, London, Macmillan, 1961.

[49] Kispista, I.: "Vélekedések az agrárgazdaságról" [Opinions on the Agriculture], Valóság, 25, 1, 80–92, 1982.

[50] Kolosi, T.: Másodlagos gazdaság és társadalmi szerkezet [Secondary Economy and Social Structure], mimeo, Budapest, Országos Tervhivatal, 1979.

[51] Kornai, J.: Economics of Shortage, Amsterdam, North-Holland, 1980.

[52] Kornai, J.: Anti-Equilibrium, Amsterdam, North-Holland, 1971.

[53] KRITSMAN, L. N.: "Geroichesky Period Velikoi Russkoi Revolutsii" [The Heroic Period of the Great Soviet Revolution], *Vestnik Kommunisticheskoi Akademii, 9,* 1925.

[54] LACKÓ, M.: "Cumulating and Easing of Tensions", *Acta Oeconomica, 24,* 3–4, 357–377, 1980.

[55] LAKI, M.: "Liquidation and Merger in the Hungarian Industry", *Acta Oeconomica, 28,* 1–2, 87–107, 1982.

[56] LANGE, O.: "On the Economic Theory of Socialism". In: B. E. LIPPINCOTT [ed.]: *On the Theory of Socialism,* New York, McGraw–Hill, 1964.

[57] LINDBECK, A.: *The Political Economy of the New Left,* New York, Harper and Row, 1971.

[58] MAJOR, I.: *Közlekedés a tervgazdaságban* [Transportation in the Planned Economy], mimeo, Budapest, MTA Közgazdaságtudományi Intézet, 1981.

[59] MARKÓ, I.: "A kiegészítő, kisegítő gazdaság szerepéről, szabályozottságáról" [On the Role and Regulation of Auxiliary Farming], *Társadalmi Szemle, 35,* 11, 36–39, 1980.

[60] MARX, K.: *Capital,* Moscow, Foreign Languages Publishing House, 1961–1967.

[61] MARX, K.: *Kritik des Gothaer Programms.* In: K. MARX–F. ENGELS: *Werke,* 19. Berlin, Dietz, 1962.

[62] MÁTYÁS, A.: *A modern polgári közgazdaságtan története* [History of Modern Bourgeois Economics], Budapest, Közgazdasági és Jogi Könyvkiadó, 1973.

[63] MOHOS, A.: *Differenciálódási helyzetkép az iparban* [Differentiation in Industry–Current Situation], mimeo, Budapest, Tömegkommunikációs Központ, 1981.

[64] NAGORSKI, A.: "Japan vs. the World", *Newsweek,* 17 July, 8–12, 1978.

[65] NAGY, L. G.–ANGELUSZ R.–TARDOS, R.: *Gazdasági közvéleménykutatás* [Economic Public Opinion Poll], mimeo, Budapest, Tömegkommunikációs Központ, 1976.

[66] NAGY, L. G.–VIRÁGH, E.: *A városi lakosság jövőképe* [How the Urban Population Conceives the Future], mimeo, Budapest, Tömegkommunikációs Központ, 1981.

[67] NYERS, R.: *Economic Reform in Hungary: Twenty-five Questions and Answers,* Budapest, Pannónia, 1969.

[68] NYERS, R.–TARDOS, M.: "What Economic Development Policy Should We Adopt?", *Acta Oeconomica, 22,* 1–2, 11–31, 1979.

[69] PAPANDREOU, A. G.: *Paternalistic Capitalism,* Toronto, Copp Clark, 1972.

[70] PORTES, R.–WINTER, D.: *Disequilibrium Estimates for Consumption*

Goods Markets in Centrally Planned Economies, mimeo, Cambridge, Massachusetts, Harvard Institute of Economic Research, 1978.

[71] Révész, G.: "Enterprise and Plant Size: Structure of the Hungarian Economy", *Acta Oeconomica, 22,* 1-2, 47-68, 1979.

[72] Simonovits, I.: *Társadalom-egészségügy és egészségügyi szervezéstudomány* [Epidemiology and the Science of Organization of Health], Budapest, Medicina, 1975.

[73] Slutsky, E. E.: "On the Theory of the Budget of the Consumer", *Giornale degli Economisti, 51,* 1-26, 1915.

[74] Soós, K. A.: "Causes of Investment Fluctuations in the Hungarian Economy", *Eastern European Economics, 14,* 2, 25-36, 1975.

[75] Szabó, B.: "Vállalati adóztatás, nyereségelvonás" [Corporate Taxation, Centralization of Profits], *Valóság, 20,* 8, 91-95, 1977.

[76] Szalai, E.: "The New Stage of the Reform Process in Hungary and the Large Enterprises", *Acta Oeconomica, 29,* 1-2, 25-46, 1982.

[77] Szamuely, L.: *First Models of the Socialist Economic Systems,* Budapest, Akadémiai Kiadó, 1974.

[78] Szép, Gy.: "Kisüzemi termelés és kisegítő tevékenység" [Small-scale Production and Complementary Activities], *Magyar Hírlap, 14,* Supplement of the Issue of 31 October 1981.

[79] Tallós, Gy.: *A bankhitel szerepe gazdaságirányítási rendszerünkben* [Role of Bank Credit in the Hungarian System of Economic Management], Budapest, Kossuth Kiadó, 1976.

[80] Tardos, M.: "Enterprise Independence and Central Control", *Acta Oeconomica, 15,* 1, 17-32, 1975.

[81] Thoben, H.: "Mechanistic and Organistic Analogies in Economics Reconsidered", *Kyklos, 35,* 292-306, 1982.

[82] Varga, Gy.: "Management—In Fast Changing Environment", *Acta Oeconomica, 27,* 3-4, 301-326, 1981.

[83] Vincze, I.: *Árak, adók, támogatások a gazdaságirányítás reformja után* [Prices, Taxes and Subsidies after the Reform of the Economic Management], Budapest, Közgazdasági és Jogi Könyvkiadó, 1971.

[84] WHO, *Glossary of Health Care Terminology,* Copenhagen, WHO Regional Office for Europe, 1975.

[85] Wooton, B.: *Social Science and Social Pathology,* London, Allen–Unwin, 1959.

Printed in Hungary, 1985
Kner Printing House, Gyomaendrőd